cash flow for
small businesses

teach
yourself

cash flow for
small businesses

teach® yourself

cash flow for small businesses
robert mccallion & alan warner

Launched in 1938, the **teach yourself** series grew rapidly in response to the world's wartime needs. Loved and trusted by over 50 million readers, the series has continued to respond to society's changing interests and passions and now, 70 years on, includes over 500 titles, from Arabic and Beekeeping to Yoga and Zulu. What would you like to learn?

be where you want to be with **teach yourself**

Orders: please contact Bookpoint Ltd, 130 Milton Park, Abingdon, Oxon OX14 4SB. Telephone: +44 (0) 1235 827720. Fax: +44 (0) 1235 400454. Lines are open 09.00–17.00, Monday to Saturday, with a 24-hour message answering service. Details about our titles and how to order are available at www.teachyourself.co.uk

British Library Cataloguing in Publication Data: a catalogue record for this title is available from the British Library.

First published in UK 2008 by Hodder Education, part of Hachette Live UK, 338 Euston Road, London, NW1 3BH.

This edition published 2008.

The **teach yourself** name is a registered trade mark of Hodder Headline.

Typeset by Transet Limited, Coventry, England.
Printed in Great Britain for Hodder Education, an Hachette Livre UK Company, 338 Euston Road, London NW1 3BH, by CPI Cox and Wyman, Reading, Berkshire RG1 8EX.

The publisher has used its best endeavours to ensure that the URLs for external websites referred to in this book are correct and active at the time of going to press. However, the publisher and the author have no responsibility for the websites and can make no guarantee that a site will remain live or that the content will remain relevant, decent or appropriate.

Hachette Livre UK's policy is to use papers that are natural, renewable and recyclable products and made from wood grown in sustainable forests. The logging and manufacturing processes are expected to conform to the environmental regulations of the country of origin.

Impression number   10 9 8 7 6 5 4 3 2 1
Year   2012 2011 2010 2009 2008

contents

acknowledgements

The authors would like to thank colleagues at MTP for their assistance in producing this book. In our organization, those involved in financial training continually share ideas and ways of explaining financial topics so that, at any time, the knowledge of one person is made up of the efforts and experience of the whole team.

Particular thanks are due to Roger Lee of MTP for his help with technical issues, for responding to the many and varied questions and for his detailed feedback on the text.

01

why 'cash is king'

In this chapter:
- the nature of cash flow
- the development of cash flow reporting
- the implications for the smaller business
- cash flow for a business start-up
- the drivers of cash flow
- cash forecasting – the key to survival

The nature of cash flow

Cash flow is the simplest financial concept of all. It is often understood best by those who know very little about accounting. If you have never been distracted by the complexities of the **Profit and Loss Account (P&L)** and **Balance Sheet**, you can more easily understand what cash flow is; *it is the real money coming in and out of a business during a particular period of time*. Cash flow movements are represented by the difference between the cash balance at the beginning of the period and the **cash balance** at the end. And because most businesses keep their cash in the bank rather than under the bed, this means that cash flow represents the change in the bank account during a particular period, be it a week, month, quarter or year.

We all understand cash flow at the personal level, or at least those of us who avoid personal bankruptcy do so! Though we may not always be effective at managing our cash flow, we understand what it means when we see that bank statement with more outs than ins and the dreaded red ink at the bottom line. We may not be able to do anything about it, but we do not agonize about what each line means, as many of us do when we first try to understand the meaning of the P&L and Balance Sheet.

So why, you may ask, is such a fuss made about cash flow and why is a 'Teach Yourself' book necessary? The answer is twofold. Firstly, because it is not enough to understand what cash flow is. Survival in the modern business world is about understanding and managing the *drivers* of cash flow. Secondly, it is vital also to understand the relationship between cash flow and the other two financial statements, the P&L and Balance Sheet, because financial success is about managing all aspects of finance in a balanced and logical way. Therefore the links between the financial statements – particularly between the P&L and Cash Flow – must be understood if the business is to survive and thrive over the long term.

The development of cash flow reporting

One major change in business thinking over the last half century has been an increase in the emphasis on cash flow reporting. Fifty years ago, external financial reports were based mainly on the P&L and Balance Sheet. There was little if any reference to cash flow, apart from the balance at the end of the period in the list of **assets** in the Balance Sheet.

Perhaps the assumption was that the Balance Sheet and P&L were all that those managing the business needed to see, that the cash position would be managed by the company Accountant's team, without the need for any external reporting processes. This belief was reinforced by the correct view that, in any case, cash flow in a particular period is highly volatile and does not reflect the short-term performance of the business, which is revealed through the P&L.

Several things happened to change this view during the early 1970s. The initial trigger was the high-profile insolvency of Rolls-Royce which led to it being put into receivership, and the widespread amazement that such a thing could happen to a large company that was reporting healthy **profits**. It led to a realization among many analysts, who should have known it already, that the numbers in the P&L and Balance Sheet require judgement and that *cash is the only indisputable reality in financial reporting*; that is, *Cash is King*. Wherever judgement is required, mis-statement – either unintentional or fraudulent – is always possible.

This began a period during the last quarter of the century when distrust in financial reporting became widespread and the concern was heightened by the impact of a period of high inflation. The impact of inflation was that profit calculations became even more judgemental and companies found that apparent profits were not reflected in cash and were therefore not available to pay **dividends** to **shareholders**.

Just after the turn of the century, the 'dash to cash' became even more marked as Enron and several other major companies collapsed at a time when they appeared to be highly profitable. The causes were many and complex but one consequence was the generally accepted view that if analysts had been monitoring Enron's cash flow more carefully rather than focusing on its profit position, they would have seen it coming.

The implications for the smaller business

During this period, the position of the small to medium sized business was quite different. Those who survived during the periods of high inflation must have known, whether from instinct, advice or common sense, that they could not run their businesses on the basis of a P&L and Balance Sheet alone. These documents, though important and interesting, are by definition produced by accountants well after the key decisions have been made. *The information that is important to run the business for short-term survival is the cash available now and the forecast of what will happen to the cash flow if intended plans are carried out.*

Of course there were many businesses that did not work this out and these were the ones that went under. There is a classic syndrome of the man or woman who buys a village shop and who borrows the money to set it up and fill it with **stock**. There is an initial euphoria as the cash flow comes in from the early **sales**, and the owner decides to take some cash out of the business for an expensive holiday to reward the family for all the hours they have put in. 'At last there are some profits to pay us back for all the hard work'!

After the holiday, there is a return to reality. The shelves are getting empty and need to be replenished, probably at higher prices. The temporary employees who have been filling in during the holiday need to have their wages paid. Cash is still coming in from sales but it is declining because the range of stock is less than it used to be. The only way of finding the cash to bring the stock back to previous levels is to ask the bank manager for more money but he wants to see a cash forecast and P&L first. Soon the windows will be boarded up and the 'for sale' notice outside.

This story reminds us of two points which we will be building on during these first few chapters. Firstly, it is the **cash flow forecast** that is the vital document for running a business. A retrospective cash flow report may be interesting and informative, but it is then too late to do anything to change it. Secondly, despite the earlier reservations about the P&L, it is an important document. It tells you how much money you are making and thus, among other things, provides guidance about how much it is prudent to take out as owners' salary or dividend.

Cash flow for a business start-up

Let's illustrate the simplicity of cash, compared to the other financial statements, by a short exercise, based on what happens to the cash position of a new start-up. It is simplified to make things easier at this stage, but its principles apply to any and every business.

J&J Foods – month one

- Janet and John decided to start a new business, selling cooked food products from their home. They invested £8,000 of their own money and borrowed £8,000 from the bank, both paid into a new bank account in the name of J&J Foods.
- They bought cooking equipment of £6,000 for cash.
- They bought £5,000 of food ingredients, paid for in cash.
- They achieved £10,000 sales in the first month and this used up all their ingredient stock.
- They allowed all their customers credit and the invoices said payment must be made within 30 days; no one had paid by the month end.
- They paid wages to temporary staff of £1,000.
- They paid themselves wages of £2,000 each in the first month.
- They went on a trip to the south of France to study food eating habits at a cost of £1,000.
- Sundry expenses were £500.

What was the first month's cash flow position?

To answer this question, we will produce a **Cash Flow statement** in its simplest form, on a cash in, cash out basis:

Cash Flow statement – month 1

	£
Cash in	
Initial capital	16,000
Cash out	
Equipment	(6,000)
Food ingredients	(5,000)
Wages	(1,000)
Salaries	(4,000)
France trip	(1,000)
Sundry expenses	(500)
Total cash out	(17,500)
Cash deficit	(1,500)

Thus Janet and John are £1,500 in deficit and the business could have collapsed before the end of the first month. Because we want to build on this exercise and show the position in the next period, we will make the – maybe optimistic – assumption that this deficit is being funded by a bank **overdraft**.

Though the cash flow of this exercise is relatively simple, the issues arising are not; they raise some fundamental questions about the financing of a business. So before we move on, let's summarize the questions raised by the exercise:

- What was the basis of their decision to raise only £16,000 initial **capital**?
- Could they, should they, have taken credit from their suppliers?
- Did they *have* to give one month's credit to customers?
- Will the customers pay within that period?
- Should they have purchased more stock by now and will the lack of stock hold back next month's trading?
- Will they need any more equipment?
- What was the basis of the salaries they drew out of the business and was that prudent?
- Will they have to pay tax?

And very important:

- Did they carry out a cash forecast for this first month?

And even more important if they are to survive:

- Will they be carrying out a cash forecast for the next month?

We will answer these questions later; in the meantime, let's set the scene by summarizing the drivers of cash flow.

The drivers of cash flow

One of the problems with forecasting, managing and reporting cash flow is its inevitable volatility. It is like a roller coaster, up one minute down the next. Indeed this is one of the reasons why the P&L is necessary and valued, because it smooths out the peaks and troughs.

To understand this volatility, it is necessary to know about the key drivers of cash flow. If we leave aside for the time being the day-to-day running of the business during which sales are made and **costs** incurred on a relatively even basis, there are some key drivers that make the cash flow so volatile, each of which will be explored in later chapters:

The collection of cash from customers

This aspect of cash flow applies to all businesses, except those who sell all their goods for cash. It is listed first because it is the least controllable. A cash flow for a period can be made to look very favourable by the receipt of a big cheque near the end of a period, or destroyed by the failure to receive such a cheque when expected. We will devote the whole of Chapter 08 to the collection of money from customers – also known as the management of **debtors** – because it is so important, probably the biggest single cause of day-to-day cash flow problems.

Stock management

Decisions about when to buy stock and in what quantities, will have a major impact on the volatility of cash flow. Such decisions often involve a finely balanced trade-off between the cost savings from bulk purchases and the costs of financing and storage of the extra stock. It also requires the asking and answering of the question – have we got the money to bulk buy? And this in turn requires the balancing of the benefits of bulk purchase in relation to other demands on cash.

Payment of bills to suppliers

Buying stock is one decision, when to pay the bill is another, and these should be seen as two separate issues. As with debt collection, it may not be entirely within your control, because the supplier may insist on a particular period of payment or even require cash upfront. But there is usually some flexibility for negotiating terms or managing some sort of delay and this can, if handled well, be an important and positive driver of cash flow. It has to be managed carefully and balanced with other factors such as supplier relationships and credit rating – Chapter 10 will provide deeper coverage of the issues involved.

Capital expenditure

Capital expenditure is any money spent for long-term benefit beyond the current year, thus representing an asset going forward. It might be land, buildings, plant or vehicles, even a licence or a software package. Accountants may make fine judgements about what is capital – and therefore in the Balance Sheet for the purpose of accounting – but from a cash flow point of view, it doesn't matter how these items are classified. They involve cash going out of the business and are usually spent infrequently, thus causing the cash flow impact to be volatile. Again forecasting is critical, because timing can and should be planned, as far as possible, to coincide with cash availability.

Major cost items

Many costs, for instance wages and salaries, are paid out regularly and evenly, which makes them relatively easy to plan for and to manage. But there are others, for instance a major expenditure on advertising or an expensive training course, which will be spent in one major outgoing, with much the same impact as capital expenditure. Again planning of timing is vital, as far as this can be determined by choice.

Seasonal impact

Most businesses have some kind of seasonal nature, though some much more so than others. The often quoted example is that of a firework company, which spends much of its year investing money until the cash comes in after 4 July, 5 November or 31 December. Interestingly, firework companies have done a good job of reducing seasonality and making fireworks more of an all the year round event, which makes their cash flow much less volatile.

The most commonly felt seasonal impact is that of the Christmas/New Year period, with cash going out to stock up beforehand, then coming in during the holiday period or, for those selling on credit, during the months afterwards. This latter point illustrates the importance of precise forecasting on a phased monthly basis; when the numbers are worked out, it usually turns out that, for those selling on credit, the period immediately after bumper sales is the worst from a cash point of view and the benefit only comes during the following quarter.

Dividends and owners' salaries

Though the split between dividend and owners' salaries of an owner-managed company may be important from a pension, or tax point of view, the cash impact is the same. It is money that you are choosing to take out of the business and must be preceded by a cash forecast which takes into account all the above outgoings and any tax on profits that still has to be paid. Once you are sure that a salary or dividend is affordable, the timing needs to be fixed in a way that balances personal needs and company cash availability. It is not being suggested that owner managers should not be paid a reasonable salary, or that shareholders should not receive a return on their investment, but the timing must not jeopardize survival of the business.

Taxation

An extension to the story of the family run village shop whose owners spent all their early cash on a holiday, is the owner who takes out all the first year's profit before tax, forgetting – intentionally or otherwise – that tax will be payable later. The rules for timing of tax payments – particularly for start-ups – are complex and depend on the tax rules in each country. Such payments will usually be once or twice a year and will be large outgoings, typically around 30% to 40% of the previous year's profits. Failure to plan for, and to be able to fund, tax payments has in recent years been the most common single trigger of company liquidation.

Cash forecasting – the key to survival

From the above it can be seen that cash forecasting is a key process for business survival, and one that is complex and challenging. However, the best cash flow forecast in the world will not *solve* a cash flow problem, it will only draw attention to it. It is the actions that follow that provide the solutions necessary to ensure survival. So the key question is: what do you do, what can you do, if the forecast shows that there is not enough cash to carry out your plans?

There are basically two options, neither of them easy: either you make choices about priorities, or you look for ways of raising more cash. The third possibility – to go bust – is assumed not to be an option. Of course some of the items above – for example, the payment of tax and, at some point, suppliers – will not be optional and others, like collection of debts from customers, will not be easy to control or guarantee. So the options are often quite limited and come down to management action around the controllable items, such as capital expenditure, stock levels and major items of cost.

However, you will always have a better chance of managing the situation if you are doing it ahead of time, following a cash forecast, rather than at the time, during an unexpected cash crisis. And, though the support of banks and other potential sources of funding will depend on many factors and can never be guaranteed, your request will be more favourably received if you have a cash flow forecast – rather than a threat from creditors – to support it.

Let's now complete the chapter by looking again at the 'J&J' exercise and answering the questions raised. We will also look forward to the next month and produce the cash forecast that is so essential for short-term survival.

J&J Foods – key questions

• What was the basis of their decision to raise only £16,000 initial capital?

It is difficult to know the basis for this key decision but they certainly should have carried out a full cash forecast so that their initial capital was enough to get them through the vital first few months. It is usually easier to get cash at the outset than to ask for more later, though clearly this will depend on the willingness of the bank to lend and the availability of own funds.

• Could they, should they, have taken credit from their suppliers?

Payment in cash has the advantage of obtaining better prices and avoiding problems of credit approval, always difficult for a new business. But the decision to buy for cash while selling on credit is bound to cause negative cash flow movement during the early stages. The cash flow forecast would have highlighted this need and included the required funding in the initial target for raising capital.

• Did they have to give one month's credit to customers?

The amount of credit to be given to customers has serious implications for cash flow but this must also be balanced with the normal terms of trade in the sector, which any new business has to take into account. If potential customers are used to taking one or two months' credit from suppliers, it is unlikely that a new business can offer anything less, unless there are substantial trade-offs. However, the important thing is that the decision is made with full information about the norms of the sector and likely customer expectations. It is also vital that the implications are included in the cash forecast.

- Will the customers pay within that period?

The unfortunate reality is that customers do not always pay on the agreed basis and this possibility has to be taken into account in any cash forecast. The problem for a new business is that it is so difficult to predict and control. Though the collection of cash can and should be influenced by efficient cash collection processes – see Chapter 08 – success cannot always be guaranteed and the cash forecast has to make prudent assumptions.

- Should they have purchased more stock by now and will the lack of stock hold back next month's trading?

It certainly does seem unwise and risky to run stocks down to zero, though much will depend on how easy it is to replenish supplies. If it is just a question of nipping down to the cash and carry, this may not be a problem. However, the general principle is that cash forecasting should take into account the need for stocks to be purchased early enough to keep the business running and without an adverse impact on customer service.

- Will they need any more equipment?

This will depend on spare capacity and the speed at which the business is to grow. Plans for extra capital expenditure should be made well in advance and timed carefully, in view of their 'one-off' impact on cash flow.

- What was the basis of the salaries they drew out of the business and was that prudent?

We highlighted earlier the importance of resisting the euphoria of the early influx of sales and of not drawing out too much cash from the business too quickly. The problem is – how do you know how much it is justified and prudent to draw out? This is where the other accounting document – the P&L – has a key role, because distributions to owners through salary or dividend must by law and by good practice, be justified by profit. This is why the whole of the next chapter is devoted to the P&L and its link to cash flow.

- Will they have to pay tax?

This final question has similar implications to the previous one and is just as important. It is vital to plan for cash to be available to pay the tax bill when it is due and that any distribution of profit has to be based on the after tax figure. However, it is also true that, where there is a significant delay in tax payments, the surplus cash can be used in the business, but it needs a careful and prudent cash flow plan to make this happen without unacceptable risk. Many businesses struggle to survive after a bad year because they are trying to pay a large tax bill from the previous year's profits out of current cash flow.

We will be developing all these issues in more depth as the book progresses. In the meantime, let's take the 'J&J' story into a second month, to illustrate the practical issues of cash flow management in a practical, and forward-looking, context.

J&J Foods – month two

Let's assume that the bank provided an overdraft at the end of the first month and that trading continued at the same £10,000 sales level for the second month, with the ingredient and running costs – including wages and salaries – also at the same level. We will also make the – maybe pessimistic but certainly prudent – assumption that 50% of customers will pay within the one month period but the other 50% will not. We will also assume that the ingredient purchases need to be increased to £6,000, to provide a 'buffer' stock for contingencies.

Cash Flow forecast – month 2

	£
Cash in	
50% of debtors collected	5,000
Total cash in	5,000
Cash out	
Food ingredients	(6,000)
Wages	(1,000)
Salaries	(4,000)
Sundry expenses	(500)
Total cash out	(11,500)
Total cash flow	(6,500)

Therefore the second month's cash balance will be:

	£
Opening cash deficit	(1,500)
Total cash outflow for the month	(6,500)
Closing cash deficit	(8,000)

Unless Janet and John have a very understanding bank or access to more capital, they will therefore go bust after only two months' trading.

J&J Foods – further questions

- What is the fundamental problem?
- What are their options to save the business?
- What further information do they now need to help their decisions?

We will continue the story into Chapter 02 and answer these questions. The theme will be the link of cash flow to the P&L and how there must be an integrated approach to financial planning.

02

profit and cash flow

In this chapter:
- the purpose of the P&L
- the structure of profit reporting
- reconciling cash and profit
- the 'funds flow' approach to cash reporting
- providing for taxation
- a summary of cash and profit differences

The purpose of the P&L

One of the questions that teachers of accounting should ask their students early on in their studies is – *what is a Profit & Loss Account for?* They should also provide the answer which, if correctly explained, will convince students of the need for a P&L and help them to understand why it is different from cash flow.

The question is important because the answer is not obvious. Why do you need this often confusing document when the Cash Flow statement is so much simpler and so much more real?

The answer is that the Cash Flow statement, for all its importance and advantages, *is not a good measure of the short-term performance of the business*. The main reasons were stated in Chapter 01: the inevitable volatility of cash flow and its tendency to be hit by 'one-off' effects that make it difficult to assess the short-term trading position.

For instance, in both of the first two months, our simple start-up example J&J Foods, had a negative cash flow. This can be proved by confirming that:

- £16,000 was in the bank at the beginning of month 1 (after the initial investment had come in).
- There was a £1,500 overdraft at the end of month 1, thus confirming a net negative cash flow out of the business during month 1 of £17,500.

In the second month there was:

- An overdraft of £1,500 at the beginning of month 2 and (assuming the bank will provide it).
- An overdraft of £8,000 at the end of month 2, thus confirming a net negative cash flow out of the business during that month of £6,500.

However, these cash flow figures do not tell us enough about the underlying profitability of the business, or how the trading positions of the two periods compare with each other. Was month 1 really that much worse than month 2? Or was it just the impact of one-off, non-recurring cash outgoings? How much profit has J&J made in each period, both before and after the drawing of salaries? This information is essential to decide how much it is prudent to draw out.

These questions require a more detailed explanation of the P&L and the answer to this key question: what is it for and how is it different from cash flow?

The structure of profit reporting

The P&L does what a Cash Flow statement cannot and was never intended to do – it measures how effectively a company is performing *over the short term*. The Cash Flow statement may answer this question over a long-term period of several years when all the 'one-off' factors have evened themselves out, but it will not do so for a month, quarter or single year.

The P&L fills this gap and it does so using accounting practices that have evolved over the years and now make up what is often known as **GAAP** – generally accepted accounting practices or principles. The most important of these principles in this context is that of *matching*. The P&L *matches* its two elements or sections with each other.

It matches:

SALES for the financial period (which may span a week, month or year)

with:

COSTS that have been incurred in generating the sales in the same financial period

to arrive at the:

PROFIT

It is vital to understand in this context that this *profit is not necessarily represented by an equivalent amount of cash in the same period*. It is also important to understand why this is the case and how the two can be reconciled. We will return to our start-up example.

J&J Foods – profitability calculation, month 1

Let's remind ourselves again about what happened to J&J Foods during the first month of trading:

- Janet and John decided to start a new business, selling cooked food products from their home. They invested £8,000 of their own money and borrowed £8,000 from the bank, both paid into a new bank account in the name of J&J Foods.
- They bought cooking equipment of £6,000 for cash.
- They bought £5,000 of food ingredients, paid for in cash.
- They achieved £10,000 sales in the first month and this used up all their ingredient stock.

- They allowed all their customers credit and the invoices said payment must be made within 30 days; no one had paid by the month end.
- They had to pay wages to temporary staff of £1,000.
- They paid themselves wages of £2,000 per month each in the first month.
- They went on a trip to the south of France to study food eating habits at a cost of £1,000.
- Sundry expenses were £500.

To work out a monthly P&L, we need two further pieces of information:

- The cooking equipment will last for two years.
- The bank are charging interest of 15% on the £8,000 loan (we are ignoring overdraft interest for simplicity at this stage).

Thus we have two extra costs that the cash flow in the previous chapter did not include:

- **Depreciation,** £3,000 per year (£6,000 spread over two years) or £250 per month.
- Interest, 15% on £8,000 = £1,200 per year or £100 per month, not charged until the second month.

It should be clear from the above extra information that another principle of the P&L is that you must include all costs, even if these have not yet been paid for in cash. The cash flow is about what has actually been paid out in cash, the P&L is about every cost that relates to the sales made during that month, even if not yet reflected in a specific cash payment. And in the case of depreciation, the calculation of that cost requires assumptions and judgements about the future, for example, how long the cooking equipment is to last.

Let's see how J&J's P&L looks for the first month:

P&L – month 1

	£
Sales	10,000
Ingredient costs	(5,000)
Gross profit	5,000
Expenses	
Temporary staff	(1,000)
Trip to France	(1,000)
Sundry expenses	(500)
Depreciation	(250)
Interest	(100)
Total expenses	(2,850)
Profit before owners' salaries	2,150
Owners' salaries	(4,000)
Loss	(1,850)

Before we look at the second month, we should make a few comments about the structure of the P&L, and its meaning and implications.

- Note that all sales are included, even though no cash has yet been received, a first and basic reason why profit and cash are likely to be different in particular financial reporting periods. The P&L includes the value of all goods and services delivered to customers in that period, whenever the cash is received.

- The inclusion of the **gross profit** sub-total is not essential but is a useful way of showing the profit generated by the basic trading function before deduction of expenses, and how this compares with other financial periods.

- The cost of the cooking equipment is not shown as the total paid out in cash but instead as depreciation, so that the impact is smoothed over several financial periods, a key function of the P&L.

- The interest is shown even though the bank has not charged it yet, because the P&L anticipates costs incurred which will be paid in cash later.

- The profit before owners' salaries is not a generally accepted level of profit but has been shown here to illustrate how the P&L could have been used by the owners to see how much they could have afforded, without putting the business into a loss position. It shows quite clearly that £1,000 a month each, a total of £2,000, would have been a more prudent payment at this early stage. It would have avoided making a loss during the first month and – most importantly – would have left the business with a positive cash balance.

Reconciling cash and profit

We should also confirm the cash flow for this same period from Chapter 01:

Cash Flow statement – month 1

	£
Cash in	
Initial capital	16,000
Cash out	
Equipment	(6,000)
Food ingredients	(5,000)
Temporary staff	(1,000)
Own salaries	(4,000)
France trip	(1,000)
Sundry expenses	(500)
Total cash out	(17,500)
Cash deficit	(1,500)

When we look at month 2, we will carry out a reconciliation that will show more clearly the differences between cash and profit in a particular period. At this stage it is enough to say that the statements are fundamentally different in purpose and will rarely arrive at the same net figure, for all the reasons stated above.

J&J Foods – profitability calculation, month 2

Having established the importance of the P&L, and the ways in which it differs from cash measurement, we will now take this further by looking at the P&L for the second month, and linking it more closely to cash flow. This is easier now, because we have a clear opening cash position of negative £1,500, represented by the overdraft.

Let's now confirm the second month's cash forecast as shown in the last chapter, and assume that these events actually take place, as follows:

- Trading continued at the same £10,000 sales level for the second month, with the same ingredient and running costs.
- 50% of customers who owed money from the first month paid by the end of the second month but the other 50% did not.
- With regard to ingredients stock, they had to buy £6,000, to provide a £1,000 'buffer' stock for contingencies.

We will assume that, based on their P&L for the first period, Janet and John have now decided only to take out £1,000 per month each as salaries. We will also include the interest for the first month, now charged by the bank. Therefore the cash flow for the second month is as follows:

Cash Flow statement – month 2

	£
Cash in	
50% of debtors collected	5,000
Total cash in	5,000
Cash out	
Food ingredients	(6,000)
Wages	(1,000)
Salaries	(2,000)
Sundry expenses	(500)
Interest	(100)
Total cash out	(9,600)
Total cash flow	(4,600)

And this is what the second month's cash balance will be:

	£
Opening cash deficit	(1,500)
Cash outflow for the period as above	(4,600)
Closing cash deficit	(6,100)

Note the difference here between a negative *cash balance* –
£6,100 – and the negative *cash flow* of £4,600, which is the
change from the opening to the closing position.

Let's now look at the P&L for month 2, based on the same
assumptions:

P&L – month 2

	£
Sales	10,000
Ingredient costs	(5,000)
Gross profit	5,000
Expenses	
Temporary staff	(1,000)
Sundry expenses	(500)
Depreciation	(250)
Interest	(100)
Total expenses	(1,850)
Profit before owners' salaries	3,150
Owners' salaries	(2,000)
Profit	1,150

The P&L looks much the same as the first month, except that
the owners' salaries are lower – for the reason mentioned above
– and the 'one-off' impact of the working holiday is no longer
felt.

The key question that now needs to be examined – the answer
to which provides the link between profit and cash – is why has
this profitable business suffered a negative cash flow of £4,600?

The funds flow approach to cash reporting

We can start to answer this question by completing a form of
reconciliation between the two statements which, as we shall see
later, is used extensively in cash reporting. It starts with the
profit position and works it back to cash flow on a stage-by-
stage basis.

Thus we start with:

	£
Profit	1,150

We will first of all add back depreciation because this is a book entry and does not involve cash, thus arriving at the profit as it would have been without depreciation being charged:

	£
Profit	1,150
Depreciation	250
Profit before depreciation	1,400

This first adjustment takes us one step closer to cash flow. We now need to adjust for the impact of sales made on credit, which are reflected in the P&L but have not yet been collected in cash. We do this by taking the difference between the amounts outstanding at the beginning of the period and the end.

At the beginning of the second month, the amount of debtors outstanding was £10,000, all of the sales of the first month. £5,000 of this was received but there has been another £10,000 sales, thus making the amount outstanding at the end of the second month £15,000. The impact on cash flow can therefore be calculated as follows:

	£
Opening debtors	10,000
Closing debtors	15,000
Negative impact on cash flow	(5,000)

Thus we can, as a second step, adjust the profit figure further:

	£
Profit	1,150
Depreciation	250
Profit before depreciation	1,400
Increase in debtors	(5,000)
Impact on cash (so far)	(3,600)

The other difference between profit and cash that needs to be included here is the increase in ingredient stock. This does not impact the P&L – because the matching concept requires the cost of stock *used* to be included – but the cash flow is impacted by the extra stock required to create the buffer.

Thus our profit to cash reconciliation can be finished off by the inclusion of the change in stock level, calculated as the difference between the opening stock of zero, and the closing stock of £1,000 (£6,000 purchased less £5,000 used).

Thus we complete this form of Cash Flow statement by a final step:

	£
Profit	1,150
Depreciation	250
Profit before depreciation	1,400
Increase in debtors	(5,000)
	(3,600)
Increase in stock	(1,000)
Cash flow	(4,600)

It can be seen that this adverse cash flow of £4,600 is the same as the actual change in the cash position as calculated in the other form of cash statement above. Thus we have completed the reconciliation between cash and profit in a way that shows the difference between the two forms of measurement, and their relationship to each other.

This is the way in which Cash Flow statements are usually presented to managers and shareholders in both internal and external reporting, because it shows the key drivers of cash flow and their link to profit within a concise and informative structure. This is such a statement in its simplest form; normally there would also be similar adjustments for changes in creditors – the amount of credit taken from suppliers – and for capital expenditure during the period.

There will be more on this format of reporting – often called the **funds flow** method – in later chapters.

Providing for taxation

It was shown above how the P&L has a role in cash decision-making, by showing how much it is prudent for the owners to take out of the business. There is also a requirement in the P&L to make a provision for taxation on profits. Though we have not yet covered tax in the interests of simplicity, a further entry in the P&L should be a **provision** – an estimate of a cost to be paid in the future – for taxation, thus reducing profits even further. The entry in the P&L would look like this, assuming 30% **corporation tax** charge and no complications:

	£
Profit before tax	1,150
Provision for taxation (30%)	345
Profit after tax	805

Though the making of a tax provision is no substitute for a detailed month-by-month cash forecast, its inclusion in the P&L does provide an important discipline. It ensures that distributions of profits are not made on the mistaken assumption that they are available to the owners, when in fact these are required for future cash payments to the tax authorities.

A summary of cash and profit differences

To close the chapter, we are showing a summary of the differences between the profit (before tax) and cash for the first two months as follows:

Month 1	P&L £	Cash flow £	Difference £	Explanation
Sales	10,000	0	(10,000)	All the sales were made on credit
Ingredient costs	(5,000)	(5,000)	0	The suppliers were paid in cash
Temporary staff	(1,000)	(1,000)	0	The wages were paid in cash
Trip to France	(1,000)	(1,000)	0	The trip was paid in cash
Sundry expenses	(500)	(500)	0	All the sundry expenses were paid in cash
Depreciation and capital expenditure	(250)	(6,000)	(5,750)	Cap ex is cash, depreciation is a book entry
Interest	(100)	0	100	Interest will be paid in month 2
Salaries	(4,000)	(4,000)	0	Salaries were paid in cash
Loss	(1,850)	(17,500)	(15,650)	

Month 2	P&L £	Cash flow £	Difference £	Explanation
Sales	10,000	5,000	(5,000)	Cash received from month 1, month 2 sales on credit
Ingredient costs	(5,000)	(6,000)	(1,000)	The suppliers were paid in cash, £1,000 of which went into stock
Temporary staff	(1,000)	(1,000)	0	The wages were paid in cash
Sundry expenses	(500)	(500)	0	Expenses were paid in cash
Depreciation	(250)	0	250	Depreciation is a book entry
Interest	(100)	(100)	0	The interest paid was the same as the month 1 cost
Salaries	(2,000)	(2,000)	0	Salaries were paid in cash
Loss	1,150	(4,600)	(5,750)	

We will now move on to cover the impact of the business model on the pattern of cash flow and its link to the P&L.

03

the impact of the business model

In this chapter:
- the business model as a driver of cash flow
- cash flow and choice of sector
- changing the norms of the sector
- examples of cash-effective business models
- a summary of cash flow drivers

The business model as a driver of cash flow

The **business model** can best be described as 'the way we do business'. It is one of the key drivers of cash flow, and one that it is difficult to influence, once you have made the choice of business sector to enter. If you choose to start a firework business, you must accept the seasonality and the need to finance the build-up of stocks between peak periods. If you decide to enter a business which requires expensive equipment or substantial research and development, you have to accept the need for investment and the high level of funding required. If you enter a business where the major competitors sell on a month's credit, you have to accept the impact of the waiting time for cash to be received.

On the other hand, if you enter a market where it is normal for customers to pay a proportion of the sales value in advance – for instance the supply of holiday packages – you will have a far lower requirement for cash upfront. And if you choose a business with very low **capital intensity** – for example, management consultancy – you will not have to find cash for an initial investment in, and later renewal of, **fixed assets**. And if you go into a retail market where cash payment is the norm, you will not have to wait for cash to come in from customers.

Let's illustrate this impact by a simple exercise that shows the difference in cash flow between two businesses; one manufacturing and supplying consumer products to the retail trade and one supplying market research services – probably to the same customers – where it is customary to receive a significant percentage of the fee in advance; we will assume a typical percentage of 40%.

We will show the difference between the cash implications of start-up and first month's trading via a simplified business example involving the two companies, assuming that each business makes £5,000 sales in the first month and has similar overall costs and profits, as follows:

P&L for both companies

	£
Sales	5,000
Direct product costs	(3,000)
Admin wages and salaries	(1,000)
Sundry expenses	(500)
Profit	500

Cash flow – Food manufacturer

	£
Cash in (sales on one month's credit)	0
Cash out	
Capital expenditure on new equipment	(3,000)
Initial stock of raw materials (assume 2 months)	(6,000)
Admin wages and salaries	(1,000)
Sundry expenses	(500)
Total cash out (and capital required so far)	(10,500)

Cash flow – Market Research company

	£
Cash in from sales (40% of £5,000)	2,000
Total cash in	2,000
Cash out	
Salaries – Market Research consultants	(3,000)
Admin wages and salaries	(1,000)
Sundry expenses	(500)
Total cash out	(4,500)
Total cash deficit (and capital required so far)	(2,500)

This requirement of £2,500 for the market research company might even be reduced by the receipt of more cash in advance of next month's sales.

Based on these assumptions, this exercise shows that the first business requires more than four times the amount of cash – £10,500 compared to £2,500 – than the second one, purely because it has chosen to enter that type of business.

We should now confirm why there is this difference, the reasons why the market research company needs £8,000 (£10,500 – £2,500) less cash to start up:

	£
No need for fixed assets	3,000
No need for stock	3,000
Payment in advance	2,000
Total cash saving	8,000

Cash flow and choice of sector

Cash flow implications should be a factor in the choice of sector to enter, but this statement has to come with a caveat. The cash flow implications might be a reason *not* to enter (say) the firework business, but they should not be a reason to *choose* to enter another business which has more favourable cash flow implications.

The driving force that should determine your choice of business to enter should be the extent to which you can create a *sustainable* **competitive advantage** that ensures long-term profitability and cash flow generation. The logical sequence of questions is therefore:

- Where do we have competitive advantage that will make the market buy our product/services rather than somebody else's?
- What are the normal cash flow implications of being in that type of business?
- Do we really understand both the long-term and short-term funding requirements of that business?
- How much money will we need to raise to be in that business?
- Can we obtain the necessary finance, either personally or from lenders, and at what cost?
- Will we be able to create enough sales and profits to pay for the costs of financing and achieve long-term viability?
- Do we understand the cash flow implications of growing the business and will we have access to the funding required?
- If not, how or where else can we find an area where we have competitive advantage?

The questions should *not* be:

- Which type of business has positive cash flow characteristics?
- Shall we therefore enter it?
- How do we create competitive advantage?

Thus the cash flow implications should be a negative factor that questions your ability to survive in a particular sector, not a positive driver that determines the sector you enter. You should be in the holiday or market research business because you have an offer that will attract customers and generate sustainable profit and cash flow, not because it will reduce your funding requirements. Otherwise there would be many uncompetitive businesses entering the holiday and market research markets and failing very quickly!

Are there circumstances where cash flow might impact the choice?

Yes, as long as the choice is within your core skills. There could be circumstances where there is a choice within the same business sector about which segment to enter: for instance someone who enters the food business and has the choice as to whether to sell food products for cash from a market stall, or to customers who are businesses and therefore demand credit. If there is a similar competitive advantage in each case and you have no other major reasons for preference, it would be logical and justified for cash flow to be a key driver of the decision, particularly if funds are limited.

If you are entering a business involving manufactured products, there may also be choices about whether you manufacture yourself or whether you subcontract to others. Again it is valid for cash flow to be a driver of choice to some extent but not at the expense of competitive advantage. If the product design and quality that you have specified is the driving force of your business idea, you must be sure that a third-party manufacturer can sustain that quality. You will also need to evaluate the cash flow implications of the terms of business that you agree with the manufacturer; if the outsourced production has to be paid for in seven days and you are selling on one month's credit, the cash flow benefits of subcontracting may not be as positive as you expect.

You also have to be careful of apparent solutions to cash flow demands that do not really change things at all. One clear case of this illusion is the decision to lease rather than buy capital equipment, a means by which managers often convince themselves that they are avoiding the fixed asset intensity of a manufacturing business. But in many cases the leases are no more than borrowing under another name and will be treated as such in the accounts. The risks and pressures will be just the same as if the asset had been purchased with money borrowed from a bank and there should be no self delusion in this respect. There will be more on leasing in Chapter 11.

Changing the norms of the sector

It is desirable from a financial point of view to change the norms of the sector if this will bring cash into the business earlier. A simple and obvious example is to ask customers for cash upfront or within seven days, whatever the competitors are offering.

Though it is clearly going to be difficult to persuade customers to agree to this, there are two reasons why start-up is the right time to do it. First, because it is difficult to change terms of business once a company has been in operation for a period, because customers and suppliers will have become used to the agreed terms of credit. Second, start-up time is when the initial capital has to be raised and it is best to get all the finance you can at the outset, rather than keep coming back for more when there is a cash flow problem.

Whether it is possible or desirable from a non-financial perspective, is another matter. Let's take as an example a business selling consumer products to major retail outlets that tries to break the mould and insist upon seven day payment rather than the normal one month. It may be possible and it certainly is desirable if it makes the cash flow position more positive, but it is taking an extremely high risk, to add to all the others that exist when a new business is formed.

The key to whether it is possible is the extent to which your product or service has competitive advantage compared to others, enough to make customers willing to allow their own cash flow to suffer in order to benefit yours. If you have a product that is so good that retailers are fighting to stock it in their stores, you may be able to change the rules of the normal business model in this way, but if you have a product that is much the same as others, or is struggling to establish a reputation or brand, such an attempt will inevitably fail. The provision of credit will be seen by most customers as one product feature, which will be taken account in the buying decision along with others.

There is also the further distinct possibility that some customers who really want your product will say yes to the seven day payment and then take much longer to pay in practice, the worst of all worlds. If your product really is strong enough to change the rules of the game in a major way, it would be better to go the 'whole hog' and ask for cash upfront or on delivery. This should test whether your competitive advantage is real!

Although it is not easy to arrange, there are examples of large customers supporting small critical suppliers by providing special credit terms or buying capital equipment on their behalf, thus alleviating the need for expensive funding. This represents a change in the normal business model that helps both small suppliers and customers. The history of the Apple Corporation describes how one retailer who believed in their product provided most of the initial finance to bring the 'Apple 1' computer to market.

Examples of cash-effective business models

Changing the business model can do more than ask for different terms of credit, it can also innovate with a completely different mode of operation. The most well known example is Dell Products, who changed the rules of the game in personal computers by a number of moves which changed not only the cash flow implications, but also the complete way of operating, for example:

- Dell deals with customers direct rather than through retailers or distributors, thus avoiding the need to give terms of credit to powerful intermediary businesses.
- They sell to customers through their sophisticated website which reduces selling costs. This enables them to make aggressive promotional offers and keeps their products competitive.
- Customers specify exactly what they require and products are made to order, thus reducing the need to keep stocks of products in the supply chain.

- They typically require payment from consumers at the time products are ordered, thus keeping their debtors low.
- They deliver the customized orders very quickly, again reducing the stock while at the same time providing outstanding customer service.
- They use third-party suppliers for many components, making their own operation mainly assembly of parts and requiring suppliers to hold the stocks of materials and components.
- They take as much credit as possible from their suppliers.

There is however an important point here. Dell's success is based on the fact that they developed a very successful business model that met customer needs more effectively, achieved rapid growth *and* had positive cash flow characteristics. The cash flow implications were not the driver of the business model but the happy consequences of it.

Has the Internet opened up new possibilities?

Very much so, particularly around the need to carry stock. Retailers who sell through the Internet can allow their customers to see an image of the product and thus replace the need for physical display, which in turn reduces the requirement for cash investment in stock of products. However, even an Internet retailer will need to hold some stock if it is to provide a prompt delivery service. The key to Dell's successful use of the Internet was their exceptionally efficient operating model that enabled them to deliver bespoke products within a few days, without the need for stockholding.

As an illustration of the impact of this strategy, Dell's average stock levels during the last few years have been the equivalent of four days' sales revenue, whereas competitors like Hewlett-Packard, Lexmark and IBM have held stocks at levels between 40 and 50 days. There is a further interesting comparison of stock levels in different sectors in Chapter 09.

A summary of cash flow drivers

It is, in many ways, better to look at the key drivers rather than the sector, because there can be variations within each sector and different companies may make different choices. An extreme case of positive cash flow would be a business which has:

- Low capital intensity and therefore limited need for capital investment
- Low upfront investment in research and development
- Customers that pay in advance
- No requirement for stock
- Supplies that can be paid for on credit.

There are certainly many examples of types of businesses that have these characteristics, for instance:

- Insurance companies
- Holiday providers
- Organizations running public training courses
- Advertising agencies
- Market research companies.

Are there downsides from a model that generates positive cash flow?

Yes there are, particularly when the positive cash flow depends on payments in advance or prompt payment by customers. The main problem is that the capital you need to raise is determined by the positive cash flow features at the time of start-up and you are therefore making the implied assumption that these features will continue indefinitely. This can leave you very vulnerable if things change, for instance if customers question the payment in advance or if competitors offer more favourable terms. A cash flow problem may also arise if there is a sales decline and the amount received in advance becomes less.

In these cases you will be faced with the need to raise more capital, which may not be timely or even possible, particularly if the business is in decline. The prudent approach therefore is to have a buffer in some form, either a cash sum in reserve or an agreed facility with the bank, which will allow enough time to raise the necessary funds.

What are the consequences for a business start-up?

That is the topic of the next chapter.

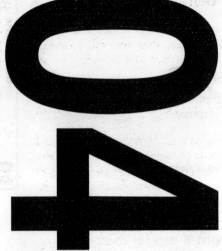

04 key decisions at start-up time

In this chapter:
- the impact of key decisions on cash flow
- issues around fixed assets
- issues around machinery and equipment
- key decisions around stock levels
- key decisions around credit to customers
- key decisions around credit from suppliers
- the combined impact of start-up decisions

The impact of key decisions on cash flow

There are a number of key decisions that we will examine during this chapter. These can be classified as follows:

- The extent of investment in assets such as buildings, computers, equipment, vehicles, and the exploration of other options if there are likely to be constraints on cash availability.
- The need for stocks of raw material, work-in-progress and finished goods to meet the needs of operations and customers
- Unless it is a cash business, the credit terms to be offered to customers, either through standard terms or, if this is the strategy, by individual customers.
- The credit terms that can be expected to be taken from suppliers of different types.
- The expenses that are likely to be needed as major outlays in the early stages in addition to the capital expenditure, for instance any upfront investment in marketing or recruitment.

It may be thought that these are mostly unavoidable consequences of a business start-up, but this is rarely the case. One principle of starting a business is that *you look at all possible options to avoid investment before making balanced choices*. The investment of cash at the beginning of a business's life is a key factor in the creation of risk; therefore the more you can avoid spending cash upfront, the more you are helping your survival prospects. But this must not be at the expense of achieving a competitive advantage.

We will now look at each of these decisions and consider the issues involved.

Issues around fixed assets

We will look at buildings first. There are a number of issues to address, summed up by these key questions:

- Do we need a building at all? This is a relevant question for many businesses in these days of on-line communication and flexible working locations.
- If the answer is yes, what kind of premises do we need to carry out our business?
- Where does it need to be located?

- Should we lease or buy and, if lease, what sort of lease should we take out?

Clearly the implications of the answers go well beyond cash flow factors so we will focus only on the financial implications. From a cash flow point of view, it is highly desirable to avoid buying or leasing a building as long as possible and, if feasible, to look seriously at the options of working from home, by virtual communications or by sharing with others. It is always best from a risk perspective, to keep the **fixed costs** – those that are incurred whatever the level of sales – as low as possible and premises cost is usually a key element of the fixed cost structure of a business.

Therefore the message must be to keep the premises costs as low as possible during the early stages, focussing only on what is essential for effective operations, knowing that you can scale up when the business has expanded and the future is less uncertain. There is a danger that budding entrepreneurs can get carried away with their new situation and go for 'gold-plating' rather than a 'minimalist' approach.

There should be similar thinking around the choice of location; where do we need to be in order to be most effective to carry out our business? Does it have to be London or in a major city? Where could we find that would be less expensive? Have we got the right balance between where we want to be and where our customers want us to be? How many of our customers will be likely to visit us?

There is no perfect answer to this choice; the key requirement is for there to be a careful thinking process which questions and challenges assumptions and eventually comes up with the most cost and cash effective option.

What about lease versus buy?

A similar logic applies to this question, and to choosing the type of lease to be taken out. This is probably the biggest potential cash investment that could be made by a new business and the thinking should be clear. *Unless you are in the property business, you should lease rather than buy, and look for the lease with the lowest possible commitment in terms of cash outlay and fixed future period.*

Some people who start a new business will decide to buy property on the basis that it is a good investment for the future, which it may well be. And investment in property may be a good financial plan for you personally. But by buying a business property you are implicitly saying that it is the best possible property investment you could make at the time. If you really want to invest in property, you should be doing so as a separate exercise, effectively a different business. Then you would have to ask yourself: is this the right time to be doing this, at the same time as starting your own business? The answer is unlikely to be yes.

There are however some important choices to be made around the type of lease to be taken out. Many new entrepreneurs have taken out 25-year leases without thinking through the implications. They may have done this because it seemed to be the best way of securing the right kind of property, but the consequences can be serious for the long term, with a commitment that hangs over for years and causes conflict and stress for those involved. Your flexibility may be restricted by the conditions of the property market at the time but the clear message should be: all things being equal, *go for a lease that is as short term as possible, with minimum initial outlay or payment in advance*. This type of lease is usually worth looking and negotiating for, even if you end up with something that is not 100% perfect, or costs more in short-term rent. Indeed, during a downturn in the property market, you may be able to negotiate an initial rent-free period because the landlord is desperate to bring in a new lessee to an otherwise empty property. You should also consider negotiating favourable breaks in the lease that give you flexibility should the business need it in the future. Again the aim must be to minimize upfront cash outlay and commitment to fixed costs.

Issues around machinery and equipment

Decisions around investment in machinery and equipment are clearly most important for a manufacturing operation, but they will impact almost every business to some extent; even the smallest business working from home will need to lay out cash to buy a desk and a computer.

But whether it is a manufacturing business fitting out a factory, or a consultant working from home buying a PC, the questions to be asked are the same:

- What capital would we ideally like to invest to run our business?
- What are the options to avoid or reduce such capital investment?
- What will be the impact of avoiding or reducing?
- On balance, what is the right choice?
- Do we have the cash to implement that choice?
- If not, what is the best option with the cash available?

We will illustrate this decision-making process with an example of best practice for a manufacturing business with a large need for capital expenditure.

The management of such a business should start by producing a specification of all the equipment needed to make the product, with no operational or financial constraints. This should then be converted into a financial estimate that we will assume calculates a total of £1 million cash required for investment. This would be based initially on the assumption that we make everything ourselves, buy new equipment and work the hours that are conventional for the kind of workforce normally employed.

The second stage is to generate options that challenge conventional thinking and the comfortable assumptions that those starting a new business often make.

Challenge one

Do we need to make the product ourselves? Could we subcontract to someone else to manufacture? What would we lose by doing this, for instance loss of control and flexibility? What would we gain by doing this, for instance the experience of an existing manufacturer?

The proper response to these questions relates to the concept of competitive advantage mentioned in earlier chapters. If you believe that you have unique manufacturing expertise that others cannot replicate, you must make the product yourself; if not, you should look for a partner to make it for you, while accepting that it is impossible to guarantee that one will be available on the right terms.

Challenge two

Are there alternative types of equipment that can do the job at lower cost? Could we buy second-hand? Are there sub-processes that can be subcontracted out, for instance the product packaging?

Again there are no perfect answers and, in the end, it will depend on whether there are feasible alternatives or whether there is a second-hand market. It is however important that the question is asked; there is a tendency for managers in businesses of all sizes to go for new equipment without questioning the alternatives and this practice must be challenged.

Challenge three

Can we reduce the cost by operating in a different way, maybe by working weekends, having double or treble shifts or asking staff to work overtime at certain periods?

The answers to this challenge are likely to involve a difficult trade-off between the likely higher operating costs of these arrangements and the reduced capital investment. In Chapter 07 we will introduce the concept of **discounted cash flow**, a technique by which such trade-offs can be evaluated in financial terms. Clearly, however, the final decision would involve more than financial numbers; there would also be issues of staff motivation, impact on product quality and the availability of people. The important requirement is for the options to be raised and considered.

The final choice

After the questions, challenges and consideration of all the options, a decision has to be made and the amount of capital investment finally agreed. This is fine as long as the cash is available. If it proves not to be available, the avoidance and reduction options must be revisited.

Assuming that the balanced judgement is that the full £1 million is needed but only half that amount of cash is available, the correct sequence of questions is then:

- What are the options that will bring our cash outlay down to £500K?
- Which of these options will erode or remove our competitive advantage?
- What are the shorter- and longer-term implications?
- Which of these options will adversely impact our running costs and therefore profitability?
- Are any of these options acceptable?

If the answer to the last question is yes, you may still have a viable business. If not it would be disastrous still to go ahead. A new business should never be started with 'make-do' solutions brought about by lack of cash availability, if these are detrimental to competitive advantage or economic viability.

What about the small business that only needs a PC and a desk?

This process is clearly less important for the business with such low capital intensity, but the principles are the same on a smaller scale and could lead to these more basic questions:

- Do I need a desk?
- Is there a second-hand desk available?
- Do I need a new computer?
- Is there a second-hand one?
- Can I use my existing PC?
- etc., etc.

Such questions would only be relevant to the very smallest start-up but it should hopefully emphasize the point: *nothing should be spent in cash until all the options have been explored.*

What about vehicles?

The same principles apply. If the business ideally needs vehicles to distribute the product, the low investment alternatives should be explored, including postage, couriers or third-party distribution.

There will also be decisions around the provision of cars for the owners and management team. These decisions will be more complex and finely balanced, involving issues of status, motivation and taxation, but again any assumptions should be challenged and debated.

Isn't the leasing of plant, equipment and vehicles another choice?

It is an important choice but one that is complex and depends on the type of lease being considered; some leases are no more than borrowing under another name so do not represent a real alternative. For this reason we will deal with this issue separately in Chapter 11, when we will look at all routes to alternative financing.

Key decisions around stock levels

We will be devoting the whole of Chapter 09 to the management of stock levels so we need only make a few points that are important at start-up time. It is however important to stress that, as illustrated in Chapter 03, much depends on the type of business. Some businesses are stock intensive, just as some are fixed asset intensive. At one extreme there is the retail store selling high-value durable items and needing to display them; at the other extreme the management consultancy that has no need for stock at all. Another variable will be the suppliers available and the speed and flexibility they are able to offer to a new customer without a track record in the business. There is a big difference between the business where standard supplies can be picked up from the cash-and-carry, compared to one that is dependant on specialist suppliers of technical components.

Though the same message applies as for fixed assets – no more cash investment than is absolutely necessary – there is an important difference; in the case of stock, any over investment can be recovered later. There is also the fact that levels of stock are likely to have a significant impact on speed of service to customers and flexibility of operation, both of which will be critical in the early stages of a business's life. The early stages will also have two other characteristics: the pattern of business will not yet have been established and levels of volume will probably be more unpredictable than at any time in its life. Thus there is a need for flexibility and quick response times.

Therefore the message to keep stock as low as possible should be balanced with the need to have a buffer stock for contingencies in the early stages, as long as the cash flow forecast takes this into account and it is affordable. When the business has developed and growth rates become slower and more predictable, that will be the time to reassess ways of minimizing stock levels, using some of the approaches mentioned in Chapter 09. This chapter will also make the important distinction between stocks of raw material, work-in-progress and finished goods, for which different criteria may apply.

A final point about stock is a reminder of the lessons from the Dell example in Chapter 03. In many retail and manufacturing businesses the level of stock required is a major driver of cash flow and can often be a constraint on the ability to start and then expand. Therefore it is important to explore options to change the business model and substantially reduce the need to hold stock, without impacting customer service or losing the essential competitive advantage. It is not easy to achieve this balance but, as Dell has shown, the rewards are high. Nor is Dell a 'one-off' in this respect. Many on-line retailers – with Amazon as the first and most well known – have managed to develop a model that achieves the joint benefits of superior service and lower stock levels.

Key decisions around credit to customers

We have already covered many of the issues involved in the first three chapters, because terms of credit are so fundamental to cash flow. There will also be further coverage in Chapter 08, along with the importance of collecting the money in line with agreed terms.

We can summarize the main start-up issue by confirming two key questions that should guide your decision-making process:

• What are the normal terms of credit in the sector where we are operating?
• Is it realistic for us to offer anything different from the norm?

The emphasis so far has been on options to improve cash flow and risk by asking for payment more quickly than the norm. Our message has been that this is unlikely to be possible unless you have a product with exceptional competitive advantage. In any case, customers often fail to pay within the agreed period, so compliance can never be guaranteed.

There is however a second 'reverse' question: is there any benefit in offering terms that require *later* payment than the norm, to improve the attraction of the total product offering? This will obviously have an adverse impact on cash flow but could attract customers who would otherwise go to competitors.

The answer here is also clear. If your product needs that incentive for customers to buy, it is almost certainly without that vital competitive advantage that is critical to long-term success. And, even more important, such a policy may attract the wrong kind of customer – those who have cash flow problems of their own and who will be most likely to delay even further, or never pay at all.

One further question at the start-up stage for those who are selling to a few major customers is – should we consider different terms for each customer or type of customer, rather than assuming one size fits all? There are strong arguments for this approach; for instance there may be large companies with reserves of cash who are willing to pay within seven days in return for a keen price and special service. There may be others whose cash flow management is built around taking a fixed number of days' credit or whose systems cannot arrange fast payment.

Key decisions around credit from suppliers

The main difference here is that you may not be in a position to make decisions because the suppliers – particularly the big powerful ones – will probably have their own terms which you have to take or leave. In the end a lot of the final decisions around credit given and taken revolve around relative power. If you are selling to Wal-Mart and buying from GE, you may not have too much choice in either case.

The simple cash flow message about credit terms to be taken from suppliers in the early stages is 'as much as possible' and, depending on the business and your own credit status, this will commonly be around 30 to 45 days. However, there is also the question of risk because, by taking credit from suppliers, you are effectively increasing your borrowing, even though the cost seems to be zero. This risk becomes obvious when the need for payment comes in 30 or 45 days' time and you have to find the money, which may not be easy if your own customers are slow in paying or if business is not developing as expected. Then there are the demands for payment and the refusals to supply which often hasten business failure.

There is also the question of the hidden cost. It may be that by taking your 30 or 45 days' credit, you are paying more cost than you need to, or forgoing a cash discount that you could have taken for earlier payment. The trade-off can be calculated before the decision is made and, provided the cash flow is flexible enough, could be a reason for not taking the credit offered, despite its cash flow benefits. The calculations involved are demonstrated and explained in Chapter 10.

The general principle to apply here is to negotiate with your chosen suppliers and, if there is flexibility, make the best choice to match your own cash flow and cost needs, within the terms that they are able to offer. However, what you should *not* do is to shop around for a supplier that will give you the credit you need to work within your cash flow limits, unless there is clearly no difference in quality of supply. The choice of supplier should be based on what is best for the product and service to customers. If more finance is needed, this is for the shareholders or lenders to provide, not a second-rate supplier.

Are there other important decisions at start-up time?

Yes, there is one more. You need to assess whether there needs to be any major upfront expenditure in the early days before cash starts coming in from customers, for instance any advertising or market research expenses that are required to generate sales, or recruitment costs to obtain staff. In Chapter 05 we will be covering the key issue of phasing cash flow forecasts month by month and this is an early example of such phased planning being required.

If such investments are essential to get the business going, there may not be much choice and the cash flow impact will depend upon whether credit terms can be obtained, but such outlays will be a critical element of the cash flow forecast in the first few months and the initial capital required.

The combined impact of start-up decisions

We will now complete the chapter by showing the different cash flow positions of two separate manufacturing businesses – one run by Jean and one run by Jeremy – that are both in their first year and have the same P&L, but who made different choices around the issues impacting cash flow mentioned above. To illustrate the difference we are quoting extreme choices as follows:

	Jean	Jeremy
Buildings	Purchased	Leased
Production	Purchased	Third-party manufacturing
Vehicles	Purchased	Third-party distribution
Stock	2 months	1 month
Debtors	45 days' credit	7 days' credit
Creditors	7 days' payment terms	45 days' payment terms

P&L – year 1

	£
Sales	500,000
Costs of production	(300,000)
Gross profit	200,000
Expenses	(150,000)
Profit	50,000

We will make the following additional assumptions:

- Cost of buildings £600,000
- Annual cost of lease of buildings £25,000
- Cost of production machinery £50,000
- Cost of vehicles £30,000
- Stock is valued at full production cost
- Sales are all on credit
- Credit purchases apply to production cost only

The differences in cash flow between the two businesses are as shown below. Calculations have been rounded to the nearest £10,000 and depreciation ignored, to keep things simple.

Cash flow impact – year 1

	Jean	Jeremy	Differences (Jeremy better off)
	£	£	£
Buildings	(600,000)	(25,000)	575,000
Production machinery	(50,000)	-	50,000
Vehicles	(30,000)	-	30,000
Stock	(50,000)	(25,000)	25,000
Debtors	(62,000)	(10,000)	52,000
Creditors	6,000	37,000	31,000
Net cash flow impact	(786,000)	(23,000)	763,000

Calculations

	Jean	Jeremy
Stock	2/12 × 300,000	1/12 × 300,000
Debtors	45/365 × 500,000	7/365 × 500,000
Creditors	7/365 × 300,000	45/365 × 300,000

Thus Jean would need almost £800,000 cash to start the business while Jeremy would need only a relatively small amount.

This example is not necessarily suggesting that Jeremy is right and that Jean is wrong. It is illustrating the main point of this chapter – that the cash flow requirement for a new start-up is crucially dependent on the above range of decisions, which must be thought through carefully in the unique context of each business.

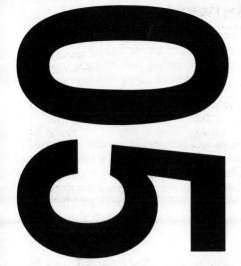

05
cash flow planning

The business plan as starting point

So far our emphasis has been almost entirely on the cash flow issues that arise when starting a business; now it is time to move on to the cash implications of running the business on an ongoing basis. The principles are in most cases very similar and the drivers of cash flow are the same, but this ongoing context allows us to say much more about the practice of financial planning.

There is no magic about financial planning; in its simplest form, it is no more than the production of financial statements in advance. The main difficulties arise, not from any technical or conceptual problems, but because forecasting ahead is a difficult process requiring sound business judgement and an effective crystal ball! But the words of Eleanor Roosevelt should be remembered at all times – 'it is better to light a candle than to curse the darkness'.

The need for planning ahead is more than just a cash flow and financial issue; it requires a **business plan** which should be a regular feature of any company's management processes and the foundation of the **financial plan**. In this chapter we will be assuming that the business and financial plans are produced annually, which ties in with the central reporting framework used by taxation and regulatory bodies in all countries. The period of a year is also the normal planning cycle and seems to work well for most sectors. However, this assumption needs re-assessing in the context of each unique business; for the very fast-moving high-tech company, a year is a long time and the shorter planning cycles of three and six months may be more valid. In any case, as we will see during this chapter, a yearly plan – particularly the cash flow forecast – has to be phased into shorter periods and re-forecast on a rolling basis as the year goes on, which allows more short-term flexibility.

The difference between a business plan and a financial plan should be made clear. Definitions, interpretations and structures vary widely between companies but the generally accepted position is that the *business plan* is a statement of what the management of the business intends to do and the expected outcomes if successfully implemented. It should be more than a statement of expected sales and costs; it should be a statement of, for instance, plans for sales and marketing activities, recruitment of new people, management of costs, investment in capital and major revenue expenditure.

Whatever format is used for the business plan, one output that must result from it is an informed estimate of the likely P&L for the period. Indeed any business plan that does not provide all the information for a projected P&L is not sufficiently focussed or complete. The P&L is the right starting point for plan projections because, as mentioned in Chapter 02, its purpose is to *measure business performance*, which must be the right focus for any business plan. The key outcome that determines the plan's viability is whether the projected sales will exceed the projected costs and whether this will make a profit that justifies being in business.

It should also be clear from Chapters 01 and 02 that the projection of the P&L is not enough financial information for a complete financial plan; there must also be a cash flow forecast. The key drivers of cash flow and the causes of differences from the P&L estimates should also be clear. As shown in the exercise at the end of Chapter 02, to arrive at cash flow, the P&L projections need to be adjusted for:

- Changes in stock levels
- Changes in debtor and creditor levels
- Investments in capital expenditure, adjusted for depreciation already charged in the P&L
- Tax payments
- Distributions of dividend

Note the reference to *changes* in stock, debtor and creditor levels. A key difference between the cash flow forecast for an ongoing business compared to a start-up, is that it is always the *changes* to these three headings, rather than the absolute value, which is important from a cash perspective.

The impact of working capital

When analysing cash flow, the three headings of stock, debtors and creditors are often grouped together as one heading. A collective term often applied to this combination of stock, debtors and creditors is **working capital** and the changes that take place in working capital during a period are usually the major difference between profit and cash flow at the operating level.

A financial plan must therefore provide a projection of the likely working capital levels based on sales estimates and any likely changes in company practices and the business environment. The following questions should be asked:

Stock

- How will the projected growth (or decline) in sales levels impact stock?
- Are we changing any of our buying and stock control practices?
- How will price increases impact our stockholding?

Debtors

- How will the projected growth (or decline) in sales impact the level of debtors? (Growth in sales will, all things being equal, inevitably cause an increase in debtors.)
- Are we changing the terms of payment for any of our customers?
- Is there likely to be a change in the time that customers delay payment, maybe because of a more challenging economic environment?
- Are we changing our cash collection practices?

Creditors

- How will the projected growth (or decline) in sales and stock levels – and therefore the amount of purchases – impact the level of creditors?
- Will our suppliers change their terms of payment?
- Will we be using new suppliers who might have different terms of payment?
- Can we pay more slowly without impacting operations?
- Can we pay more quickly and make cost savings?

Once these questions have been answered and estimates made of stock, debtors and creditors at the end of the period, the working capital impact on cash flow can be confirmed.

The calculation would look like this:

	Opening position	Estimate at period end	Impact on cash
	£	£	£
Stock	1,000	1,200	(200)
Debtors	1,500	1,750	(250)
Less creditors	(600)	(800)	200
Working capital	1,900	2,150	(250)

Note that working capital is the *net* investment after creditors have been deducted from stocks and debtors; in other words you are using the credit from your suppliers to offset the cash you have to invest in stocks and debtors. Thus an *increase* in creditors – which you would normally expect to happen when sales, stocks and debtors are increasing – will have a favourable impact on cash flow and reduce the net impact of working capital from a potential £450 (£200 + £250) down to £250.

The impact of capital expenditure

The impact of capital expenditure is much more straightforward. All you need to do in your cash forecast is to estimate the cost of the capital spending specified in your business plan, using the tests around potential avoidance or reduction that we discussed in the previous chapter. Capital expenditure is not included in the P&L so the profit figures must therefore be adjusted when arriving at likely cash flow outlay.

There also needs to be an 'adding back' adjustment for depreciation as shown in Chapter 02. Assuming that no other factors are causing differences between profit and cash, the cash flow would look like this:

	£
Profit	1,150
Depreciation (already deducted from profit)	250
Profit before depreciation	1,400

And then a reduction for the amount of capital expenditure:

	£
Profit	1,150
Depreciation (already deducted from profit)	250
Profit before depreciation	1,400
Capital expenditure (say)	(400)
Cash flow projection	1,000

Thus it can be seen that the net impact on cash flow is the *difference* between depreciation and capital expenditure; the more your current year requirement for capital exceeds the depreciation from previous years, the more the impact on cash flow will be negative. This is not necessarily a bad thing for the business, indeed it is likely to be a feature of growth, but the funding has to be available. There should however be concern if capital expenditure exceeds depreciation when growth is not taking place, unless there is a clear strategic reason for investment.

Linking profit and cash plans

From the above it can be seen that a quick way of showing the impact of fixed assets on cash flow is to take the net difference between capital expenditure and depreciation, in this case £150.

This difference, plus the change in working capital, provides the main link between cash and profit at the operating level, though the important 'below the line' items of tax and dividend are still to come. There may also be special non-trading items that are not covered by the above headings, for instance payments to pension schemes or rents received from sub-letting properties.

This approach allows us to display the link between profit and cash – and therefore the cash flow forecast – in its simplest form. For example, using the above figures for both the main headings:

	£
Forecast profit	1,150
Depreciation (already deducted from profit)	250
Forecast profit before depreciation	1,400
Capital expenditure (say)	(400)
	1,000
Forecast increase in working capital	(250)
Operating cash flow forecast	750

Or even more concisely:

	£
Forecast profit	1,150
Net increase in fixed assets	(150)
	1,000
Forecast increase in working capital	(250)
Operating cash flow forecast	750

The netting off of both fixed assets and working capital in this way allows us to see the variables in simple terms and to summarise the cash flow implications of a business plan in one concise statement.

The two key drivers that can cause a profitable business to have cash flow problems are increases in net fixed assets and working capital. Increase these and your cash flow generation will be less than profit; reduce them and you will generate more cash than profit.

Taxation payments

When we bring in taxation, the relatively simple link between cash and profit breaks down, because taxation is not simple and the timing of payments is critical to cash flow forecasting. The cash flow implications of tax are further complicated by the fact that there are different kinds of taxation in different countries and the rules about the amount to be paid and the timing of those payments will vary enormously.

There are three main types of tax and they are all important for cash planning purposes:

• Corporate tax levied on **operating profits**, usually at a rate that varies between 25% and 40% (there will often be special adjustments to the operating profit for a number of factors, a complexity that is outside the scope of this book).

• Sales or **Value Added Tax (VAT)**, levied on the amount of sales and typically paid quarterly in arrears.

• Taxes connected with employment, both amounts deducted from salaries and employers' contributions.

We will cover only corporate tax at this stage, as it is the only tax payment which has an impact on longer-term cash flow planning. The other two categories are more relevant for short-term, month-by-month planning and will be dealt with in this context later in this chapter.

Assuming that the corporate tax rate is 30% and that it is paid in the same year as the profit is earned, the example cash flow forecast below can be completed as follows:

	£
Forecast operating profit	1,150
Net change in fixed assets	(150)
	1,000
Forecast increase in working capital	(250)
Operating cash flow forecast	750
Corporate tax (30% on £1,150)	(345)
Net cash flow forecast	405

However, in most cases, it is not as simple as that. The forecast for tax payment will need to be based on the *actual tax paid during the year*, a potentially complex calculation that requires specialist tax advisers to confirm the method of tax computation, the timing of payment and any options for flexibility. The delay of tax payment is not generally recommended as a way of helping your cash flow position but advisers will tell you of the limits to which you can legitimately go and of any interest or penalty charges that might be incurred.

The dividend decision

The dividend is the final figure to make up the cash flow forecast which can now be completed as follows:

	£
Forecast operating profit	1,150
Net change in fixed assets	(150)
	1,000
Forecast increase in working capital	(250)
Operating cash flow forecast	750
Tax to be paid	(300)
	450
Dividend to be paid (say)	(250)
Net cash flow forecast	200

The timing of the dividend payment is different from the other outlays as it can more legitimately be delayed, as long as the shareholders are consulted and are agreeable. It is also true that one purpose of the cash flow forecast is to find out what dividend it is possible to pay in the forthcoming period. If there is insufficient cash to pay the dividend, and no acceptable way of solving the problem, the shareholders have to accept that delay or non-payment is in the interests of the business.

The decision to pay a dividend is a complex one which requires balanced judgement. In a small business managed by its shareholders, that decision will also involve personal needs and preferences, and the owners' tax position. At the other extreme, top management of a large public company have to be seen to be acting in the interests of the shareholders and the decision about dividend is one of the most challenging and controversial of all, particularly when times are hard.

What factors impact a decision about dividend levels?

The questions to arrive at a balanced decision illustrate this complexity and show how the cash flow forecast is central to the decision:

- What profit after tax have we made in the most recent period?
- What are the cumulative distributable profits that are available to be paid? There are legal constraints which define the profits that can be distributed by a business to its shareholders.
- What dividend did we pay last year? A dividend cut from the previous year is seen as a very negative factor by shareholders and has to be justified.
- What can we afford in the short term? In the above case the company can clearly afford no more than £450 and maybe less if seasonal phasing is taken into account.
- What can we afford in the long term? This will ideally require a business plan and cash flow forecast beyond the current year; clearly it would be wrong to pay the whole £450 if there is likely to be major capital expenditure in the following year.
- What further finance could we, should we, raise in the future, both this year and in following years? It is possible that the capital expenditure could be funded by borrowing or further shareholder investment if this is in the interests of the business.
- How confident are we of our forecasts and what buffer do we need to hold in cash to avoid taking unacceptable risks? Clearly a decision to pay dividend should not allow the

survival of the business to be in doubt and the management has to weigh this factor against the preferences of shareholders and their own view of risk

The length and complexity of these questions shows that this is not a decision to be taken easily or lightly. This happens too often, particularly during the early stages of a business's life when an inexperienced management team see cash being generated and are too hasty in wanting to take it out. At the other extreme, management teams in more mature companies are sometimes criticized for being reluctant to pay a dividend when surplus cash is clearly available, because of a desire to minimize risk and keep options open.

Management's job is to get the balance right and a cash flow forecast is the essential requirement, not just for the coming year but a longer-term forecast into the future.

Short-term cash planning

There are three broad timescales for a cash flow forecast:

• Short-term – month by month
• Medium-term – over the next year
• Long-term – over the next several years

Short-term cash flow planning needs a different, more itemized structure, compared to the format covered in this chapter so far.

It requires detailed month-by-month projections of the cash you think will be received and paid out over the next two or three months. One of the benefits of modern technology is that what used to be a time-consuming chore can easily be produced on a standard spreadsheet using a simple program that should be within the scope of the average computer user. So if you are not capable of simple spreadsheet programming, a key requirement for a business start-up is to find someone who is. We will come back to this issue in Chapter 13 when we cover the recruitment of financial expertise.

We recommend a regularly updated quarterly cash forecast, split between the three months, as an essential requirement for any business. A cash forecast for any longer period within the year should be covered by the monthly phasing and updating of the annual plan.

For the quarterly cash forecast it is not appropriate to use the framework covered earlier in this chapter. For *short-term* cash forecasting, you need to go into more detail, taking the headings of the P&L and converting them into their cash equivalent. For instance, your P&L will contain the following headings:

- Sales
- Cost of sales
- **Operating expenses**

Whereas the short-term cash flow forecast must contain these headings:

- Cash collected from customers
- Cash paid to suppliers for goods and services
- Cash paid for operating expenses – including wages

In practice this means that your cash flow forecast has to have the following subsidiary questions and calculations:

Cash collected from customers

The key questions are:

- How much of current debtors will pay this month, next month, the month after, not at all?
- For sales taking place next month, how much will come in the same month, how much the following month etc?

It will, in many cases, be impossible to answer these questions in month-by-month, customer-by-customer detail so simplifying assumptions have to be made, for instance that cash collected will be the same as sales of the previous month, or that collections will be equally phased over the period. You have to be sure however that these assumptions have been thought through and are the best possible ones you can make because, although collections from customers are the most difficult cash flow of all to forecast, it is the area where getting it wrong has the most serious consequences.

Cash paid to suppliers of goods and services

Key questions also need to be asked here:

- Are we planning any stock increase that would have an impact on purchases?
- Are we planning to change the way we pay our suppliers?

The advantage compared to cash collections is that at least the payment of suppliers is within your control and you should be able to make sure that payment is made according to agreed terms.

Cash paid for operating expenses

The questions here are:

- Are there any 'one-off' outlays during the next three months, for instance an advertising campaign or a training course?
- Will any new employees be taken on?
- Will wages be paid regularly month by month or will these be distorted by bonuses?

Another point to bear in mind when converting operating expenses into cash flow form, is that depreciation should be excluded, because it is not a cash outlay and will therefore not impact a cash flow forecast.

Tax payments during the period

The questions here are:

- What will be the payments of sales tax/VAT in the period, based on estimated sales and costs, and when will payment be made?
- What payments of employees' income tax deductions will need to be made and what will be the timing of these, taking into account any allowed delay that would impact the month-by-month figures?

So what will the three-month cash flow forecast look like?

You will also need to bring in the other cash flow items that are not part of day-to-day operations – capital expenditure, corporate tax payments and dividend – assuming that there is a cash flow outlay during the three-month period.

There is no standard format but we are suggesting that the spreadsheet should look something like this:

Quarterly cash forecast

	Month 1 £	Month 2 £	Month 3 £	Total quarter £
Sales receipts including VAT	1,800	1,900	2,300	6,000
Other receipts	30			30
Total receipts	1,830	1,900	2,300	6,030
Cash paid to suppliers	1,080	1,100	1,150	3,330
Wages	400	400	440	1,240
Taxes on wages	100	100	100	300
Dividends	–	250	–	250
VAT payments	80	110	130	320
Corporation tax	–	–	300	300
Capital expenditure	100	–	200	300
Other payments	10	20	–	30
Total payments	1,770	1,980	2,320	6,070
Net cash flow	60	(80)	(20)	(40)
Opening cash balance	250	310	230	250
Closing cash balance:	310	230	210	210

The key figures to monitor on the forecast are the *opening and closing balances for each month* because these tell you whether you need to look at options to cover any cash deficit or, if things are going well, to consider investment of any temporary surplus. If the three-month forecast is showing a serious deficit that could jeopardize survival, urgent action is required, either to fill the gap with temporary finance such as an overdraft, or to look at options to reduce cash outlays. We will be discussing the use of overdrafts in more depth in Chapters 06 and 14.

How often should you produce a three-monthly cash forecast?

It should be maintained on an ongoing basis. This is why the spreadsheet is so necessary; it makes it easy to keep the three-month forecast going all the time, with updates at each month end, replacing the previous forecast with the actual cash balance and projecting forward another month.

This kind of quarterly forecast is important for any business but absolutely essential for those with particularly sharp seasonal peaks and troughs. We mentioned in earlier chapters the extreme example of the firework manufacturer, but seasonal factors apply to almost any business to some extent. Those selling chocolates will see enormous peaks around Easter and Christmas, with a sharp drop over the summer months; ice cream suppliers on the other hand, will have a summer peak.

Longer-term cash forecasts

We have already mentioned the importance of an annual cash flow forecast, linked to the business plan, using the format shown earlier in this chapter. There should also be a monthly or quarterly split to gain even earlier information on likely seasonal phasing issues.

The need for cash flow planning over even longer periods will depend on whether top management see any benefit from planning further forward than a year and this, in turn, will depend on how far there is a clear vision and strategy into the future. Many businesses survive without a long-term plan, preferring instead to play things by ear and allow growth to happen, responding quickly to events and to customer needs. A lot will depend on the stage of development, the type of business, the rate of change and the level of uncertainty; there is no point in long-term planning if it is impossible to make accurate projections.

If there are long-term plans beyond the current year and these can realistically be converted into financial terms, the projection of cash flow is relatively straightforward. Using the same framework as was introduced earlier in the chapter, a five-year cash flow might look like the example at the top of page 63.

	Year 1	Year 2	Year 3	Year 4	Year 5
	£	£	£	£	£
Forecast operating profit	1,150	1,300	1,500	1,700	2,000
Net change in fixed assets	(150)	(100)	(200)	(400)	(250)
	1,000	1,200	1,300	1,300	1,750
Forecast increase in working capital	(250)	(300)	(350)	(400)	(450)
Operating cash flow forecast	750	900	950	900	1,300
Tax to be paid	(300)	(350)	(400)	(450)	(525)
	450	550	550	450	775
Estimated dividend	(400)	(450)	(475)	(500)	(600)
Net cash forecast	50	100	75	(50)	175

One advantage of this method – and some might say a concern in terms of realism – is that you need not go into the full detail of the P&L, which may not be possible so far ahead. You will need to forecast approximate sales growth to arrive at likely fixed asset and working capital changes but all you will require to arrive at profit is a broad assessment of likely profit margins, not line by line cost estimates. This approach to cash flow planning allows you to say in broad terms that, if you grow profits and invest agreed amounts in working capital and fixed assets, you will generate a certain amount of cash for your shareholders. As mentioned earlier, this type of forecast should be an important factor in the dividend decision and should ideally be carried out before that decision is made.

In this example, top management might decide that the dividend payment assumption, though justified by profits, is not leaving enough surplus cash to cover potential downside risks in the first four years.

Such long-term cash flow forecasts often stop at the sub-total before dividend (£450 in year 1), to show the amount that is potentially available for shareholders over a long period, often termed 'free cash flow'. Such estimates are frequently made by stock market analysts when looking at business valuations based on future cash flows, which will be explored further in Chapters 12 and 15.

What is the secret of accurate sales forecasts?

There are no secrets, not even any techniques; it is mainly about having a clear business plan and knowing your market well enough to forecast likely volume of business. It's about knowing your customers and your competitive advantage, thus having a realistic grasp of the sales that you can achieve in the relevant period. Sales forecasts should not start with a number or a percentage, they should start with an understanding of the market and your position in it.

In businesses with a high level of uncertainty, there may be a case for sales and cash flow planning at two or three levels:

• Pessimistic
• Realistic
• Optimistic

The first two will probably be enough for most businesses from a cash flow point of view; however the optimistic scenario can be useful as a motivating stretch target to aim for. Looking at the pessimistic level – the worst possible downside forecast that can be foreseen – allows you to prepare for the worst with a contingency plan, or a stand-by overdraft arrangement with the bank.

The pessimistic scenario should also be accompanied by a related estimate of costs; in most cases there would be decisions to reduce costs – and capital expenditure – if sales proved to be well down on plan and these should be factored into your pessimistic cash scenario.

06 sources of funding

In this chapter:
- the main sources of funding: debt and equity
- sources of equity funding
- loan capital
- types of loan agreement
- requirements for loan finance
- real-life stories

The main sources of funding: debt and equity

There are two main alternative sources of funding but, within that framework, a number of options. The alternatives are the choice between two fundamentally different forms of finance – **debt** and **equity** – which we need to explain before we look at the options in more detail.

Debt finance is money borrowed from people or institutions that are willing to lend you money, on which you will have to pay interest. The bad news is that this interest has to be paid whether or not you make profit; the good news is that the lenders are not in any way owners of the company and will not be entitled to voting rights or dividend.

Equity finance is money obtained from investors to whom you are, in return, giving a share of the ownership. The implications are the reverse of the above; the bad news is that you have to share dividend with them when profits are made; the good news is that they cannot insist on such payment if profits are not being made.

This fundamental difference should be the basis of the choices you make once you know how much cash is required to run the business and, in principle, it should be determined by your attitude to risk. The key questions are:

- Do you want to go for the low-risk option of a large proportion of equity, which means that you have no fixed commitment to pay interest when times are hard and only have to face disappointed shareholders?
- Or do you want to go for the high-risk option of a large proportion of debt, which means that you will have to pay a fixed cost but, if things go well, you will keep all the remaining profit yourself?

This is in practice a choice that you may not be able to make because often, when a business starts up, it is more a question of what finance you can get. There will be limits on the extent to which people and organizations are willing to invest in both equity and debt, particularly in the early stages when you have still to establish a track record. And, at the start, it may already have been determined who will be the equity shareholders and the shares they hold, based on the way the business came into being.

Sources of equity funding

The first factor in determining the level of equity funding is how much the founders of the business are able and willing to put in themselves, and the extent to which this amount is enough for the initial capital requirements. Unless the new business is one with very low cash requirements or the founders have large personal wealth, it is likely that some extra funds will be needed. There are then broadly two choices: to invite family and friends to take some equity, or to gain access to **'private equity'** investors who are willing to put money in as shareholders rather than lenders.

For both options there are important issues to be taken into account. Keeping the investment within the family and friendship circle is comfortable and, in some cases, relatively easy. There is likely to be more personal trust and flexibility than will normally be found among external investors. But the key question is: do you want to jeopardize family relationships and friendships to the potential strain that may well be caused by such arrangements?

It should be realized that this strain doesn't only happen when things go wrong, there is no dividend and maybe their investment is lost. Resentment can also occur when a business goes very well and the working owners, and their fellow employees, see investors receiving large amounts of money for – as they may see it – doing nothing. Such conflict can, it is true, also occur when the shareholders are all working in the business and efforts are seen not to be equal, but it is even more likely to happen where there are absent investors. As time passes by, the memories of the circumstances of investment will fade and the motivation of those working in the business can be seriously impaired.

The alternative is to go for 'private equity'. This term has become very high profile in recent times, because of much publicized bids to buy major companies such as Boots, Sainsbury's and Debenhams and take them from public into private ownership. In fact this is just one type of activity that falls under the private equity umbrella. Far bigger in terms of number of deals are those private equity investors who are willing to invest in start-ups and small businesses who need cash to expand. Sometimes these investors are wealthy individuals looking for opportunities to invest in companies with growth prospects; sometimes they are companies who specialize in this type of investment.

As with money from friends and family, there is an upside and a downside. The upside is that the investor will almost certainly ask some fundamental questions about the business and the risks involved. This is a healthy process because, assuming the usual quality of the people involved, you know that if you get the money you have a viable business plan. The other benefit of private equity investors is that they are likely to give you the sort of sound business advice that is invaluable, particularly if you choose one who knows the business sector. You will also find that others in the business – particular senior employees without equity investment – will be far less resentful of the return made by external shareholders of this kind, than they will be of absent family shareholders.

The main downside is that such an investor will require a sizeable chunk of the equity in return for the investment and you will have to make a big sacrifice of potential dividend and capital growth, compared to what you would pay in interest to a bank. Remember however the other potential benefit mentioned above: such investors get nothing if the business fails, hence their desire for a return that covers this risk.

Another likely implication of having equity investors of this kind is that, once they are on board, they will want to tell you how you should be running your business, whether or not you want such advice. And they may very quickly become assertive if things begin to go wrong. In many cases this will be in the interests of you and your business but it has to be accepted as an inevitable consequence of taking the private equity route.

Where do you find private equity investors?

This is a real challenge because it is not the sort of service that advertises itself or where you can look in the *Yellow Pages*. If you are lucky enough to have friends and acquaintances who move in the same circles and know of investors who would be interested in your business, you should meet those that are recommended. You might also obtain recommendations from your bank manager, as part of the general advice to look for – see Chapter 14.

The best recommendations usually come from those who have been down a similar road and this is but one example of something that should be a key priority for any budding entrepreneur – a strong network of business contacts within your sector and local environment. There are many routes that you may consider – Chambers of Commerce, Breakfast Clubs, Trade Associations – and you will benefit in many ways from discussing issues of common interest. In particular you should be able to find positive recommendations for private equity investors. Usually such people and organizations specialize in investments of certain types, size and sector, so you need to seek out business people who will have had a similar requirement in the past. Even if the first potential investor you meet is not interested or does not fit your profile, it is likely that you will receive advice about your chances and recommendations about who else to approach.

What are the chances of obtaining private equity investment?

This depends entirely on the strength of your case, and the process is a good test of your business viability. Some of the questions we have asked in earlier chapters – in particular, what is the competitive advantage and how far is it sustainable? – are precisely the questions that will be asked by a potential investor of this kind. They will also expect a sound understanding of the financials in terms of likely cash and profit forecasts, and the assumptions behind them.

If you can put over your plans clearly and convincingly, and show yourself able to answer the challenging questions that will inevitably come, you should find this test to be easier than you expect. If you are not confident of doing this it is probably best not even to try, and therefore not to ask for investment of this kind. Those who have seen reality television programmes like *Dragon's Den* – where prospective entrepreneurs have their ideas challenged and sometimes their financial cases destroyed – will have gained an impression of what such an ordeal can be like. Such programmes can naturally exaggerate the reality and show extreme positions but they still represent sound guidance about the sort of questions asked and attitudes taken. Private equity investors' first priority is to make money for themselves rather than to help you in your career, and you have to accept this reality if you seek their support.

When should you give equity to employees?

This is an important and difficult issue, the implications of which go way beyond this book. The answer is complicated by the tax position in most countries because 'giving' equity will be likely to create a tax liability for the recipient, even if a profit has not been realized in cash. It is therefore possible that an employee may not want such a gift, particularly if it is a private company for which there is no market to sell into. There are special tax-approved share option schemes which allow employees to buy shares at an advantageous price but employees may not have the cash or may not want to make such a lasting commitment to the business.

On the other hand, there is no better way of retaining employees and obtaining their long-term commitment, if you can somehow find a way round these problems. One alternative is some kind of 'shadow' scheme whereby valued employees don't take shares but are paid dividend as if they were shareholders at a particular level, the amounts being paid as bonus through the normal reward system.

One further factor to bear in mind is what happens when an employee with equity decides to leave the business; it is not a pleasant situation to have a former employee, maybe even a competitor, holding shares in your business. Unlike loans from the bank which can be repaid, equity finance is for ever, unless an exit can be managed within a legal framework. There are therefore two important golden rules; only ever give equity to employees whom you want to keep for a long period into the future; even more important, hire a good lawyer to draw up a well thought through and watertight shareholder agreement that allows such shares to be transferred or cancelled when that person leaves the business for any reason.

Loan capital

Loan capital is often seen as the best form of finance because it avoids the downside implications of giving away equity, as mentioned above. But, just as with equity, loan finance has advantages and disadvantages. The main advantage is that you are not giving away any of the rights of ownership and, as long as you pay the interest on the loan and repay it when agreed, you will not normally have investors telling you how to run your business. Obtaining a £100,000 loan from the bank can lead to a few years of commitment to a fixed rate of interest and a tough repayment schedule; obtaining a £100,000 investment in equity can lead to someone else owning 30% or 40% of your business for ever.

The reality is that loan capital is the best form of finance for the existing shareholders if things are going to go well in the first few years and you can cover the fixed cost and repayment commitment involved. Equity is the best form of finance if you are going to struggle in the first few years and need the flexibility that comes from only having to pay dividends if and when profit is made. The problem is that, at the time, you do not know which scenario is going to apply so you have to make a balanced judgement, based on what is available and at what cost, your perception of your business prospects, and your attitude to risk.

Where do you go to obtain loan capital?

The first and most obvious source is your normal bank. We will talk in Chapter 14 about the importance of the banking relationship and how you might choose your bankers. We will assume here that a normal banking relationship has already been established prior to the request for loan finance.

It is vitally important to go to your bank manager – accompanied by a financial adviser if necessary – with a well prepared case, showing how much finance you need and over what period. This should already have been established via the business plan and cash flow forecast discussed in earlier chapters.

For reasons which should be apparent from earlier chapters, it is likely that there will be two separate needs which should be clearly stated in your loan request:

- Some relatively permanent loan capital with a repayment schedule that covers cash flow needs over the first few years, to cover the capital expenditure and permanent working capital required to achieve your business plan.
- A short-term borrowing or overdraft facility which you can draw on to an agreed maximum as required, to cover seasonal requirements, other peaks and troughs and unexpected happenings.

There will be different rates of interest for the two forms of finance and, in both cases, it is most common for these to be of a variable nature, thus making changes in the economic environment an additional risk of taking the loan capital route. The interest rate for permanent loan capital will normally be lower than the overdraft rate but will not necessarily cost you less in the long run. The advantage of the overdraft – and its key benefit from a cost point of view – is that you only take it when you need it and the interest is chargeable on a daily basis. Once you have committed yourself to loan capital you receive the money and pay interest on the full amount from day one, even if it is just lying in the bank

Types of loan agreement

There are many different types of loan and the bank will work with you to find the terms that match your needs most closely. There are three main categories which will have differences in terms of:

- Basis of rate fixing
- Amount available
- Loan period
- Whether **capital repayment 'holidays'** are possible
- Charges for early repayment

The chart opposite shows the different types of loan and the likely conditions attached.

A loan agreement can be a long, complex document. It is important to remember that almost everything is up for negotiation and aside from discussing basic issues such as the due date of the loan and the interest rate, you will also need to establish the loan fees and ensure flexibility to pay off your loan earlier than the due date while incurring minimum penalty. You should negotiate a grace period for your payment schedule and check to see that late payment charges are reasonable.

Because of the complexity, there may be a case for obtaining advice from a finance broker who will explain, in detail, the main terms of different types of loan and help you to choose the most suitable type and lender for your needs. They will also agree to negotiate the deal for you, though it is also important to do your own homework, and be able to guide the negotiation.

Is it likely that you will have to provide security?

Yes it is highly likely, whether you are talking about a permanent loan or an overdraft. You have to bear in mind that the typical high street bank is not likely to lend money to a new business unless the amount is fully covered by secured assets;

	Base Rate Loan	Fixed Rate Loan	Treasury Loan
Interest rate	Variable – the rate you pay will change as base rate changes.	Fixed for the whole period of the loan. You will therefore know exactly what the repayments will be every month. Your rate will remain the same even if base rate falls.	Fixed or variable – repayments tailored to your cash flow. If you choose a fixed rate your rate will remain the same even if base rate falls.
Loan amount	From £500 to £500,000.	From £500 to £100,000.	Over £100,000.
Loan period	Between 1 and 20 years.	Between 1 and 10 years.	Between 1 and 25 years.
Capital repayment holidays	May be taken in the first two years.	Not available.	Monthly payments can be tailored.
Early repayment charge	None.	For loans over £25,000 a fee may apply if you choose to repay part or all of your loan early.	The fixed rate is calculated on the full term of the loan, so a fee will apply if you choose to repay part or all of the loan early.

they are not in the business of high-risk, speculative lending. In some cases the assets of the business may be sufficient as security, for instance if you have already bought a business property that exceeds the value of the loan. In most cases however the assets of a start-up business will not be adequate as security and the bank will be looking for personal assets, in particular a residential property. It is likely that your own house will already be secured to a mortgage lender and you will need to take legal advice about the options.

In the event of security of this kind being unavailable, some banks will be satisfied with an agreement to give them first claim on the company's fixed assets stock and debtors, before the claims of other creditors.

It should be stressed however that security alone will not guarantee a loan from a bank; they only want to resort to security as a fallback position. Banks will only lend money if they believe that you are capable of covering interest and repaying on the agreed date, which means that they must believe in you and your business idea.

Requirements for loan finance

In summary most lenders require you to:

- Show that you can find a significant share of the capital to finance your business – ideally up to the same amount as you want to borrow. Demonstrating that you have taken on personal financial risk to set up your business will prove to a potential lender that you are committed to its success.

- Show that you have contingency plans for repayment of the loan if things go wrong.

- Offer maximum possible security, including as many personal and business assets as possible as collateral for the loan.

- Keep lenders informed of your business situation, particularly any changes or problems.

- Come over as a convincing business person. The overall personal impression you make to a potential lender is also vitally important. They may scrutinize your educational background, your business experience, your personal reputation and your employees. The evidence is that the smaller your business, the more closely you are likely to be evaluated at the personal level.

- Prepare a comprehensive business plan, with full P&L and Cash Flow, and be prepared to talk convincingly around it if required.

What are the chances of obtaining an unsecured loan?

A lot depends on your track record and your reputation with the bank but generally the chances with your normal high street bank are quite low. It also depends on the amount you want, the economic climate and the business you are in. It is therefore worth shopping around if you think that your business case is strong; in some cases a bank that believes in you might be willing to take a chance if you are willing to move your accounts – both personal and business – over to them.

There will also be other banks apart from those in the high street that might be more likely to invest in an unsecured loan, if a strong business case can be made. You will however have to pay a higher interest rate for such a loan and the approach will be similar to the search for private equity; you will need to find out the names of likely lenders through your network and must be able to produce a compelling business case.

Another option in the UK is the possibility of obtaining a Small Firms Loan Guarantee (SFLG). This scheme helps to overcome the problem of small business funding by providing lenders with a government guarantee against default in certain circumstances.

The SFLG is a joint venture between the Department for Business, Enterprise and Regulatory Reform (BERR) and a number of participating lenders. Participating lenders administer the eligibility criteria and make all the commercial decisions.

The main features and criteria of the scheme are:

- A guarantee to the lender covering 75% of the loan amount, for which the borrower pays a 2% premium on the outstanding balance of the loan.
- The ability to guarantee loans of up to £250,000 and with terms of up to 10 years.
- Availability to most UK businesses with an annual turnover of up to £5.6 million and up to five years history, with only a few restrictions.

Real-life stories

The stories that follow illustrate the pros and cons of debt versus equity, and how the different choices turned out well for three famous UK companies.

Body Shop

Anita Roddick started her Body Shop business as a single shop in March 1976. She and her husband could not raise enough capital to stock the shop so they asked a personal friend, Ian McGlinn, to invest £3,000. They decided to give him a significant proportion of the equity rather than commit to interest payments so early in the life of the business.

McGlinn continued to hold between 20% and 25% of the shares and to collect the same proportion of dividends, retaining his shares even when the company went public.

It says something for the people concerned that there was no apparent resentment from the Roddicks or from their staff. They accepted the consequences of giving equity and that their friend was getting a reward for the risk he took.

When Body Shop was sold to L'Oreal in 2006, McGlinn received £137 million, £20 million more than Anita Roddick and her husband!

Morrisons

Ken Morrison wanted to open his first supermarket in 1961. He had no security to offer but thought he would try his luck with the local banks anyway. He tried a few and then, to his surprise, struck it lucky: a Midland Bank branch manager saw something in him and agreed to provide a £70,000 unsecured loan. Ken was on his way to starting a supermarket chain that eventually acquired Safeway and is now valued at around £8 billion. He retained all the equity in the family until he went public, and required no further funding from the bank after the loan was repaid.

Marks & Spencer

The families of Marks & Spencer inherited from the original founders a belief that the business should be funded by equity rather than by debt. It was an old-fashioned risk-averse attitude, but it was what they believed in. The family received a lot of criticism during the 1970s and 1980s as analysts said that they should be paying higher dividends and borrowing money to allow quicker expansion and higher returns. After all they had the best security that could be offered – valuable retail properties.

In the 1990s and early 2000s, the company lost its way as the family failed to make succession plans. One factor in the company's ability to survive that crisis period was the lack of fixed interest commitment, and the security of property that was not encumbered by debt. This allowed the new management much more flexibility when they came in to launch their highly successful recovery plan, which took the company back to something like its glory days.

07

controlling capital expenditure

In this chapter:
- definition of capital expenditure
- attitudes towards capital and revenue spending
- planning and control
- evaluation of capital projects
- a story of financial control

Definition of capital expenditure

In the first five chapters we discussed the main factors that drive cash flow and are likely to cause a profitable business to have cash flow problems. Two factors dominated the coverage: the control of *working capital* – the net total of stocks, debtors and creditors – and the impact of investment in *capital expenditure*. Each element of working capital will have a chapter devoted to it but first we need to say more about capital investment.

The definition of *capital expenditure* is any amount spent on assets which have a benefit beyond the current financial year and are not therefore treated as immediate costs in the P&L, but are included as assets in the Balance Sheet. This definition contrasts with costs that *are* included in the P&L – often referred to as **revenue expenditure**. The argument for treating capital expenditure differently is that it would distort the calculation of profit to charge the full amount as a cost, matched against the sales of one single period. If, in 2008, you buy a machine to last your business for ten years, it would be misleading to match the full amount as costs against 2008's sales and therefore charge against profits.

Capital expenditure by this definition can be anything that has a long-term benefit, both **tangible** – those that you can touch – and **intangible assets**, such as **acquired goodwill** and intellectual property. However, accounting rules dictate that, with a few exceptions, intangible assets that have long-term benefit are generally treated as costs. For instance amounts spent on research, advertising and training, which are almost by definition long-term, are normally written off as costs in the P&L.

Therefore our coverage of capital expenditure in this context is mainly around the type of tangible assets that a business might buy for long-term benefit. The typical list of such assets in a mature business is likely to be:

- Land and buildings
- Plant and machinery
- Computer and office equipment
- Furniture and fittings
- Vehicles

In most businesses the amount invested in these items is significant and will have a major impact on cash flow, in both the short and long term. The extent to which this is the case is often referred to as 'capital intensity': the more a business is capital intensive with large and regular needs for capital investment, the more it will make demands on cash flow. A major factor in managing cash flow is therefore to make sure that any capital investment is justified, essential and only made after looking at all the options. It is also important that, where capital is invested, it is well controlled and effectively utilized in the business.

Are there grey areas in the definition of capital?

Yes, very much so. The definition of long-term benefit is one that is very much subject to judgement. We have already mentioned the issue of intangible investments like research and advertising; there are also difficult judgements around whether major renovations are to be treated as capital or are taken to the P&L. For example, if a factory machine has broken down and is renovated to improve performance, how much should be treated as a repair (revenue) and how much as improvement (capital)?

In practice, such grey areas are dealt with through each company's accounting policies, which are agreed with the auditors and then applied consistently to similar transactions and over successive financial periods. It should be realized however that this judgement does not in itself impact cash flow; it only impacts the type of cash flow statement described in Chapter 02, which starts with profit and works back to cash. Indeed, one of the advantages of cash flow measurement compared to the other financial statements is that it is not impacted by accounting judgement; whether you call a major renovation or research expenditure capital or revenue, it still impacts the cash in the bank account in just the same way.

Attitudes towards capital and revenue spending

Attitudes towards the two types of spending depend upon the company and the context and are often different, which is something to be avoided; the message that both types of expenditure are just as important in cash flow terms should be delivered loud and clear. In practice the different attitudes can work in two different ways.

In the first case, many companies insist upon comprehensive authorization processes to accompany capital expenditure, with a detailed form requiring a statement of strategy and risks, together with an evaluation of the benefits. These are normally very healthy processes because they require management to think carefully and offer sound justification before investing large amounts of money in assets that provide long-term benefit. The only criticism of such processes is that they can slow things down and become too bureaucratic; they can also sometimes be used for investments in relatively small amounts of money, just because they are classified as capital.

The real problem however is that such authorization processes are often forgotten when similarly large amounts of money are invested in revenue expenditure, for instance on advertising, training and research. Just because they are treated as revenue expenditure and are charged to the P&L, there is much less scrutiny and a much more casual decision-making process. These investments are just as much cash flow as similar amounts spent on fixed assets and should also have appropriate evaluations of strategy, risks and cost/benefit.

The second example of different attitudes is in the way the two types of expenditures are controlled within the financial planning system. In this case, the position is usually the reverse of the above. Once budgets have been approved and the year is under way, there is regular monthly scrutiny of costs in the P&L compared to budget, with lots of analysis of variances and updating of the latest cost and profit position. On the other hand, the **capital budget** is often treated differently, as if it were not real money, just some separate fund that does not have any real impact on profit. Therefore money can be spent at any time without too much care about whether or not it is in the budget.

It is true that such behaviours are typical of the larger, more bureaucratic companies but the small business should be careful of similar attitudes creeping in; the message should be that investment of major amounts of money requires cash and, however it is treated from an accounting point of view, it still requires rigorous evaluation and control.

Planning and control

At the time the annual plan is produced, there should, in addition to a P&L forecast, be a clear statement of the capital investments that are to be carried out during the next 12 months, listed item by item. This list should be as specific as possible, not vague estimates like 'office equipment £1,000' or 'furniture £2,000'. If the decision process is that vague, the amount should be challenged and made more specific; otherwise the best assumption may be that the money should not be spent.

The list should also include the best estimate of the time of year when the money will be invested. This timing should initially be based on the ideal time from an operational point of view, but may have to be modified once the phased cash flow – as described in Chapter 05 – has been prepared. If the ideal time to spend the money coincides with the time when seasonal stock increases are needed and corporate tax has to be paid, there will be a need to review and possibly adapt to likely cash availability.

We show below an example of how a typical listing of capital budget items might look:

Budgeted Capital Expenditure

		Estimated unit costs £	Total cost £	Cumulative balance £
Early January	5 Dell Computers, Inspirion, for the administration office	1,250	6,250	6,250
Mid February	2 replacement sales vehicles – Vauxhall Fastgo	15,000	30,000	36,250
Late March	1 replacement Xerox copier, ZX 3500, for the copying department	12,000	12,000	48,250
Mid April	3 additional delivery vehicles – Vauxhall Loto	15,000	45,000	93,250
Late June	Wrapping machine for packing area – model 79534	30,000	30,000	123,250
Early September	Purchase and installation of ventilation system for office block C	26,750	26,750	150,000
Total annual expenditure				150,000

It may be that, at the time of the plan, the final decisions about whether to buy or which type to choose have not yet been made, but there should, in that case, be the best possible estimate. It is important to remember when preparing a capital budget, that this is not the final decision-making process; just because an item is on the budget list, it does not mean that there is an all clear to buy. There must be a later stage of final decision-making that has all the necessary details and options, and considers the financial justification of the investment.

As regards control, there are three issues that are critical. Firstly, there should be as much flexibility as possible around timing, even beyond what has been assumed at the time of the annual plan. This may depend to some extent on how far the investment is necessary to continued operations and central to budget assumptions but, assuming that there is some flexibility, it is important that timing is managed in line with agreed cash limits. Capital expenditure is usually the most discretionary and postponable outgoing in the budget and can therefore be a useful lever to trade off against the unpredictability of other cash drivers.

The second issue around control also impacts timing. It is the need to delay, if possible, major capital expenditure until the time of year when it becomes clear whether other budget assumptions, particularly around sales levels, are to be met. It was mentioned in Chapter 05 that there should be contingency plans for more pessimistic levels of sales achievement and it is quite likely that these plans will involve the delaying or cancelling of capital expenditure and other major outlays, particularly if the investment is related to assumed higher sales volumes. It is therefore vital not to commit too early and thus lose the flexibility to cancel or postpone if necessary.

Finally, there is the simple but important need to compare the planned capital budget with the actual amounts spent, to check that expenditures are being kept within the plan and that any trade-offs or overspends are managed. This applies particularly to major plant or building projects which run over a long period and can easily run out of control. Another example of the difference between the treatment of capital and revenue expenditure is that, whereas there are lots of published comparisons and revised estimates of actual to planned P&L items, there is normally much less information about the capital budget.

A well-controlled business should be producing something like this:

Actual and Budgeted Capital Expenditure
at 30 June 2008

		Budgeted expenditure £	Actual cost £	Variance analysis £
Early January	5 Dell Computers, Inspirion, for the administration office	6,250	5,750	500 Favourable
				Lower average cost negotiated
Mid February	2 replacement sales vehicles – Vauxhall Fastgo	30,000	32,000	2,000 Adverse
				Higher vehicle specification agreed
Late March	1 replacement Xerox copier, ZX 3500, for the copying department	12,000	0	12,000 Favourable
				Expenditure deferred until September
Mid April	3 additional delivery vehicles – Vauxhall Loto	45,000	45,000	Nil
				Purchased in line with budget
Late June	Wrapping machine for packing area – model 79534	30,000	29,000	1,000
				Quoted price discounted by manufacturer
Early September	Purchase and installation of ventilation system for office block C	26,750	26,750	

Evaluation of capital projects

Evaluation methods depend a lot on the amount of investment and the type of benefits that are going to be provided. There are however some key questions that were mentioned in Chapter 04 and which should be central to any evaluation:

- Do we *have* to spend this money?
- What are the alternatives?
- Are there ways of avoiding it?

Businesses that are capital intensive have higher cash outgoings and are more likely to have cash flow problems; hence the 'spend nothing' alternative should always be considered. There are businesses that become addicted to capital expenditure, whose managers come to regard an investment in assets almost as a virtue in itself, and such attitudes must be challenged. A similar attitude also encourages managers to buy the new, gold plated version of whatever equipment is required, rather than examining lower cost alternatives.

The first key factor in determining the method of evaluation is the amount involved. If the proposal is for a relatively small amount in the context of the business – say less than £500 for the small business – it is usually enough to rely on business judgement and common sense cost benefit analysis. If the amount is more significant, the approach will depend on which of two types the expenditure falls under:

- Is it an investment for which there is no direct financial benefit, something that is needed for reasons that are essential to doing business, for instance an investment in safety equipment or replacement of office furniture to create an acceptable working environment?
- Or is it an investment for which there is an obvious direct and tangible return, for instance new machinery to generate more sales volume, computer equipment to reduce administration costs, new trucks to reduce maintenance costs?

The first category requires the same approach as the small investment, a common sense appraisal of the costs and intangible benefits, but with the same questioning process mentioned above. There must be an examination of all the alternatives, including doing nothing, and a full assessment of any less expensive way of achieving the same objective. It should also be realized that, although many such investments are justified, there must be a limit on expenditure of this kind, because otherwise the profitability of the business, through the increasing depreciation charge, will decline over both the short and long term.

If it is the second category, and there is a quantifiable benefit directly arising from the investment, there should be a more rigorous analysis. The type of analysis can take many forms and is likely to ask the following key questions:

- How long will it take to pay back?
- What value will be generated?
- What return will we make?

Some of the techniques used to answer these questions are relatively complex, for instance the calculation of **Net Present Value** and **Internal Rate of Return** – see later. However, all the evaluation techniques have one thing in common: they require an evaluation of the **incremental cash flows** that arise directly from the investment. By this we mean the change in the bank account as a result of that decision to invest, which might be:

- Cash savings on repairs or staff overtime
- Cash generated from extra sales
- Cash from the disposal of other assets

These incremental cash flows should be evaluated over the lifetime of the asset and then compared with the cost of the investment.

We can use an example based on the simplest of all the evaluation techniques – the **payback** method. This method requires a calculation of how quickly the money from the investment is returned. For example, let's assume that you buy a new machine that is more efficient, will cut out overtime and will allow you to sell off your existing machine. Assuming that the machine has a five-year life, the cash flow might look like this:

				Cumulative position
		£	£	£
Purchase of machine			(100,000)	(100,000)
Year 1	Sale of existing machine	5,000		
	Overtime savings	20,000	25,000	(75,000)
Year 2	Overtime savings		30,000	(45,000)
Year 3	Overtime savings		30,000	(15,000)
Year 4	Overtime savings		30,000	15,000
Year 5	Overtime savings		30,000	45,000

This evaluation shows that the payback of cash flow comes during the fourth year. The initial £100,000 investment was a negative cash flow and the right-hand column shows the cumulative cash flow position of the project as it progresses and makes savings. In year 1, £25,000 comes back so there is £75,000 left to be paid back before the project breaks even. At the end of year 3, there is still a £15,000 shortfall so it is only half way through the fourth year that the cash is paid back.

This method of evaluation is widely used, though one of its weaknesses is the difficulty of establishing what is the required level of payback – for example, in this case, is 3.5 years good enough? Of course the answer is that 'it depends' on the nature of the project, the type of business you are in, and the other projects that you might invest in; each company has therefore to set its own standard. It is however reassuring to know that the project pays back within its assumed life and this knowledge becomes part of the strategic judgement about the desirability of investing.

The other weakness of the payback method is that it does not take account of the financing costs of funding the £100,000 in the first place, or of the positive impact on financing costs of the money coming back in later years. This is where the more rigorous methods of evaluation come in, by converting the future cash flows to their present value, based on the average cost of capital – what are often known as DCF or Discounted Cash Flow Techniques. For those who would like to know more about how these techniques are used, there is an explanation in the Appendix – see page 171.

A story of financial control

Control Software was a highly successful business by any standards. It was a start-up less than ten years ago and had found a highly profitable niche in the provision of software packages that support the financial control of the business. Their growth had been steady rather than spectacular during the first few years until the aftermath of the Enron scandal – and the new Sarbanes Oxley reporting regulations in the US – made improved financial control a must for US quoted companies.

The founding partners were very quick to see the opportunity and to produce one of the first products that was tailored to the needs of the new control environment. Sales grew dramatically over the first few years of the new millennium and profits grew even faster. The founders reasoned that this was a business that was not capital intensive so the majority of profits were paid out as dividend to fund their ever grander lifestyles, leaving very few cash reserves.

The founders did however have concerns about the financial control of their own business. In particular they were concerned that the managers they had recruited did not have a cost-conscious approach to running the business. They would spend money on marketing, travel and entertaining without caring how much it cost; they all knew that sales were growing significantly year on year, that the profit margins were ever higher and that any planned profits were likely to be exceeded.

This encouraged the founders to appoint for the first time a Financial Controller; previously all the people employed in the financial area were involved in production of financial statements; there was little emphasis on cost control. Another reason for the employment of a Financial Controller was that for the first time there was to be a major capital project – the move to a new headquarters which would be built on a green-fields site purchased during the previous year, financed by a mortgage from the company's ever supportive bank. The founders agreed that they would forego a major part of their dividends for the next two years to pay for the development of the site.

The recruitment of a Financial Controller was carried out by a leading recruitment agency, briefed to find someone who worked in the control area for a top company. They came up with a highly impressive young man – qualified as an MBA and as an accountant – and he spent the first few months putting in a sophisticated system of financial control, based around the P&L, with managers being given strict expenditure limits, regular updates and calculations of variances against plan. Managers suddenly became more cost conscious, though they complained about the lack of freedom to spend money on attracting new clients. However the cost headings on the P&L were all kept at the same levels as the previous year, and in line with planned limits.

The founders were relieved to be able to relax and not to worry about financial control and they spent an increasing amount of time on the site of the planned new headquarters, dealing direct with the architects and designers. It did not seem to occur to them that the cost of the new headquarters project was at least five times the amount of the marketing, entertaining and travel costs for a single year. During almost every visit they asked for 'gold-plated' changes to the specification which progressively increased the project cost.

The founders reassured themselves that they had a Financial Controller who was looking after cost control, and who would also keep track of the changes to the project specification. Unfortunately that message did not get through to the Financial Controller. He had come from a big company background where cash flow and major capital projects were dealt with by other departments; his expertise was purely around control of the P&L.

The company continued to grow its sales and the P&L showed that the company had its most profitable year, just as the marble floor of the new reception area was being completed and the fish tanks delivered.

The liquidators were called in just a week before the new headquarters was due to open.

08

debtors and cash collection

In this chapter:
- factors determining debtor levels
- credit to overseas customers
- the importance of cash collection
- influencing customers to pay
- other actions to minimize debtors
- processes for approving credit
- effective and ineffective approaches

Factors determining debtor levels

Perhaps the most important factor is the trade terms that are initially agreed with customers, as discussed in earlier chapters. There are choices to be made but you have to be realistic in what you ask for, and what you can expect to be delivered. You can ask for payment within seven days – or even immediate payment in cash – but clearly this all depends on the custom and practice in the trade, what your competitors are offering and whether the customer is really going to deliver.

The more the payment terms are out of line with industry norms, and what the customer would normally take from its suppliers, the less likely you are to get payment on time. So a key factor in fixing payment terms is to set realistic goals.

There are a number of factors that determine what is realistic and one of the most important is the country of operation. In the UK, normal terms of payment have traditionally been in the region of 30–45 days, yet in southern Europe – for example Italy and Greece – the norms have been longer, often as much as 60–90 days. Yet further north – for instance, Germany, Holland or Scandinavia – the terms would tend to be shorter, more like 15–30 days. It is interesting however, that with the increasing internationalization of business, the terms of the different European countries seem to be converging in recent years towards a 30–45 day norm.

These are however generalizations that will usually be over-ruled by the norms of the sector, for instance market research suppliers will normally ask for a significant percentage to be paid in advance of any work being carried out.

The important requirement for someone starting a business is to know the norms, have a clear but realistic policy and plan cash requirements accordingly.

Should there be a consistent approach to all customers?

This will depend very much on the profile of your customers, in particular how many you have and their relative size and power. If you are in the retail sector, this is probably unlikely to be an issue because normally everyone will pay in cash or by credit card. If you are selling to lots of small businesses, it is unrealistic to think of each customer separately and, unless there are special factors, you should agree terms that are typical for the industry sector, similar to those that competitors are likely to be offering.

If however you are selling only to a few major companies, then you can look at each customer separately, because the terms of payment are an important part of the deal. The starting point should be the normal terms of trade in the sector but you may decide to offer something different as part of the value package, to meet the special needs of that customer.

You should however be very wary of offering longer payment terms to attract new customers. Firstly, it will appeal most to those customers who are short of cash and who may be potential bad debts. If your product or service gives good value it will sell without this kind of incentive. Secondly, such a policy will have a serious impact on your cash flow and will cost you in terms of interest to be paid or foregone.

There is a simple calculation that shows the impact on your interest costs. All you have to work out is the number of days extra that you are offering and assume a typical bank borrowing rate, which we will assume as 12% per year for simplicity. If you are offering an extra month's credit to the customer for a £1,000 order, the 12% per year is 1% per month and so the equivalent of an extra £10 per month cost to you. Thus you should be charging at least 1% extra – £1,010 – for each extra month of credit. However, bear in mind that you will have to find the cash in the first place and that you may be helping to create an eventual bad debt. The longer you have to wait for payment, the more likely it is that you will never receive it.

The same calculation can be made for the offer of a cash discount for prompt payment. In the above case – still assuming an interest rate of 12% per year – if you are offering a 1% discount to bring forward payment by less than a month, you are losing out. If you are offering 2% – which is quite common – you will have to bring forward payment by two months to make it economic. This is why most companies always take the cash discounts that are offered. It is also why you should be very careful about offering one, unless it is part of the pricing package you are offering to the customer, thus taking it beyond a purely financial mechanism.

You should also bear in mind that many companies take the discount and still do not pay on time, which puts you in a difficult position, unsure whether to spend time making a fuss about a relatively small amount.

Credit to overseas customers

When supplying overseas customers you need to take account of different circumstances. When agreeing price and payment terms a number of factors, in addition to the usual considerations, need to be taken into account, for example:

- Goods generally take longer to get to the customer, for example a shipment to Australia may take over six weeks to arrive. Applying standard terms of payment would probably mean that you would be asking your customer to pay for goods before they arrive – not something they are likely to be happy about.
- This longer delivery time will mean greater exposure to risk, because there will be several orders in transit before the cash is received from the first sale.
- If you are invoicing in the customer's currency, this risk will be increased by the exposure to foreign exchange movements.
- Distance, time zones and language may mean that collecting cash from customers can be more difficult and time-consuming.

When making sales overseas there are benefits from using **Letters of Credit** to limit exposure to risk of non-payment. A Letter of Credit is a form of payment guaranteed by a bank which will allow you to obtain payment earlier, in return for a discount taken by the bank. This is particularly useful for large contracts; however these can be complex and you have to ensure that you are complying with the terms and that the banks involved are reliable.

Another option is to ask your customer for a **Bank Draft**, which is a much simpler way of using the banking system to organize payment. The basic principle is that the paperwork required to enable the goods to pass through customs is made available through the banking system, but only when the customer has confirmed instructions for payment.

Letters of Credit and Bank Drafts are specialized areas and you should consult closely with your bank before bringing these into customer negotiations.

Another option to reduce risk is credit insurance, which is available in various forms. Although it is an expense that will reduce your profits and should therefore be taken into account when negotiating the price, it will give you greater reassurance and certainty. An insurance specialist should be able to provide you with further information on costs, restrictions and likely terms.

The importance of cash collection

There is little doubt that failure to collect cash effectively is a major cause of insolvency in business. It is usually the number one driver of short-term cash flow because it determines when sales from the P&L become 'real' and have a positive impact on the bank account. It is potentially a simple process yet one which many companies – particularly those in the early stage of development – fail to deliver.

There are a number of reasons for this. Firstly, it is a difficult, messy and sometimes embarrassing process. Entrepreneurs and sales people love closing the sale and keeping a good relationship with their customers but do not like the less exciting process of trying to get money out of them a month or so later. Secondly, it is not easy to find the right channel of communication, because it may need contact with the accounts department with whom it may be difficult to develop a relationship. And finally there is the key question of relative power, to which we will return when we cover creditors in Chapter 10; you may not have the ability to insist that payment terms are adhered to, when faced with the traditional excuses for delay, such as:

- The invoice has gone for authorization and has not come back.
- The computer has broken down.
- We do not have an order number.
- We've never seen it.
- You are not an authorized supplier.
- There's a query/error that is holding things up.
- We always pay at the end of the month.

And of course:

- The cheque's in the post!

There are no magic answers about how to respond to these type of excuses; it all depends on each situation and relationship. However there are some important principles.

First and most important is to provide no excuse for delay. You should find out at the earliest possible stage if a purchase order number – increasingly common these days – is required. If one is required, make sure that you find this out before delivery of the goods or service, or at least before sending the invoice.

Even more important, do everything possible to avoid errors or ambiguities at the invoicing stage by making sure that your customer understands completely what you intend to invoice and the amounts involved. It is sometimes tempting to leave the wording as vague, particularly if you are 'trying it on' – for instance to recover expenses where there is some ambiguity as to what is chargeable. However this is usually counter-productive and just leads to delay at the payment stage. Customers – who are managing their own cash flow – will usually take up any opportunity to delay payment, so you must avoid providing them with easy excuses.

Influencing customers to pay

Whatever the relative power situation, someone in your organization has to do everything he or she can to develop a good relationship with the people in the customer offices who actually deliver the payments – normally different people from those who make the buying decision. You must get them on your side, help them to see things from your point of view, point out the importance of cash flow to your business and how you need cash to continue to deliver the goods and services that you supply.

If you are a small business and the customer is a large one, it is quite legitimate to make the point that cash flow is important to your survival, though you must be careful not to give the impression that you are desperate – even if you are! If your customers are also small businesses, then you should be looking to establish mutual understanding, while being firm and assertive about your own needs.

In practice there will be enormous variations in customer responses and a lot will depend on the extent to which they have a clear policy and efficient systems. The best operators will usually be very clear and assertive about the agreed payment terms and stick to them rigidly, with a system that is designed to deliver in the number of days agreed. The worst operators will be less clear, will maybe have different policies for different parts of the business, will delay payments when they have a cash flow problem and will probably have inefficient payment systems.

Between these two extremes, there will be many shades of grey, which you can influence by the relationship you develop and focus that you provide. There may be some occasions when it is appropriate to get tough and to threaten consequences if payment is not made by a certain time. In general however a threatening attitude should be a last resort when all else has failed, when it is clear that you are not being treated fairly, and when the relationship is likely to end anyway. But in those circumstances such an approach should only be used when it is the best way of getting the money quickly, rather than making you feel better. People in charge of payment of invoices in companies are not usually intimidated by threats and have choices about whom they give priority to; an over-threatening style may just make them dig in their heels and keep you waiting even longer.

Other actions to minimize debtors

We have already mentioned the importance of accurate invoicing to avoid the need for queries; the other closely related factor is speed of invoicing. The simple but often overlooked fact is that invoices are normally paid a certain number of days after they are received, or within an invoicing processing run, whenever the goods or services are delivered. So produce invoices quickly and you will receive quick payment. There may have to be a carefully managed trade-off here; on occasions the need to produce an invoice quickly may have to be at the expense of accuracy and judgement has to be applied to get the balance right.

You should also bear in mind that many companies pay invoices at the end of each month and there is something here that you can do to encourage early payment. If you know that a company pays at the end of a month, or if that is the pattern that emerges, you should make sure that you put through all possible invoices before the month end date, otherwise you will need to wait another month to collect.

In the end however, the secret of effective cash collection can usually be summed up in two words – focus and persistence. When the business gets to a certain size it may be possible to appoint a full-time collector of cash, often called a credit controller or credit manager. The best people of this kind are those that regard collection of cash as a crusade and who are constantly reminding customers, persistently and firmly, by phone and by e-mail, that payments must be made on time. Those responsible for payment will soon get the message and arrange for on time payments.

If you are not big enough to employ someone like that, the answer is simple, you do it yourself or you nominate someone – in a small business usually your senior financial person – to see this as a high priority for part of their time. Too often companies only chase customers for cash when they have time after other priorities have been dealt with; or even worse when serious cash flow problems arise. It should be a high priority of your nominated person to keep regularly in touch with debtor levels and ensure that overdue payments are chased.

This person should be supported by regular information on debtor levels, the most important information being a list of debtors outstanding, with those that are overdue highlighted and analysed by age and therefore by seriousness. A company with good control ought to be able immediately to answer these questions:

- How much money is owing to us in total?
- How much of this is overdue?
- How much is more than one month overdue?
- How much is more than two months overdue, etc?
- When did we last make contact with the major offenders?

The person with the responsibility for debt collection should be supported by those who make the sales, but only if this improves the likelihood of success. If the person chasing for payment has a good relationship with the invoice payment department, this may not be helpful or necessary. But if the delay in payment is due to the sales contact not releasing the invoice, or if the invoice payment department seem to be deliberately unhelpful, there may be a case for getting the sales person or team involved. The key question is: will it make payment more likely? If all it does is upset the normal sales contact or those in charge of invoice payment, it might be counter-productive.

Certainly those responsible for sales should take an interest and be available to help if required, seeing it as a team effort. They, and everyone in the business, should regard a sale as not finally complete until the cash has been collected.

Processes for approving credit

Credit approval is a subject that is much wider than cash flow and could justify a book on its own. It is however true that there is a relationship between credit approval and cash collection, though it is not as direct as some people believe. For instance it is true that many 'blue chip' companies, who will get a **triple A credit rating** and will never ever go into liquidation, are notoriously slow payers, either because it is their policy or because they have inefficient systems. It is also true that the company that pays you quickly is not always the one that will survive in the long term; they may be paying you quickly just to keep supplies coming in and will do so right up until the day they go bust.

Nevertheless, any bad debt is a serious blow to a business and it is important to do everything you can to check the credit rating of customers that you are not sure of. There is no point in wasting time on credit checks on the Unilever and BPs of this world but there are generally accepted processes for companies or individuals that are less secure.

Depending on the type of customer, these are:

- Credit checks through your bank to the customer's bank.
- Enquiries through well-known credit agencies like Dun & Bradstreet, which will include any previous bankruptcies and County Court judgements.
- Taking out references from other suppliers.

None of these checks are foolproof but they will usually give you sufficient information to decide if you are taking a risk and if that risk is worthwhile. This evidence should be combined with your own intuition about the standing of the company, which must be objective at all times. Sometimes sales people who are anxious to make a sale may bury their heads in the sand when the issue of stability and creditworthiness comes up. In particular you should be worried if a company is very keen to do the deal and you are not sure why they are choosing you. If it is all too easy, there is probably a reason – they have tried everyone else!!

If the credit rating comes back as adverse, there are two options. One is to walk away from the deal. It is important that you are not talked into giving credit despite the credit rating, by the various excuses that dodgy companies are likely to make. For example – 'that was many years ago' or 'we had a dispute but it's now been resolved'.

The other option is to ask for payment in advance or on delivery, which will help your cash flow and test out the customer's wish to do business with you.

Effective and ineffective approaches

Things that people in *effective* cash flow companies will say:

- 'We need a clear understanding about terms of payment so that we both know where we stand.'
- 'Who is the person in your organization to contact about invoice payments?'
- 'I am sure you will understand that our ability to continue to deliver service to you depends on our cash flow coming in as planned.'
- 'Is there anything more we can do to help you make our payments according to the agreed terms?'

Things that *effective* cash flow companies will do:

- Invoice quickly.
- Invoice accurately.
- Make contact with the person who decides when payments are made.
- Develop a harmonious relationship, based on mutual understanding.
- Approach the customer immediately that payment is overdue.
- Involve sales colleagues if this is likely to help.
- Keep plugging away, politely and persistently, until the cash comes in.

Things that *ineffective* cash flow companies will say:

- 'We are quite flexible about when our customers pay.'
- 'Don't bother about our financial people, they do chase too keenly sometimes.'
- 'If we keep asking for payment on time, we might upset them.'
- 'If we query their credit rating, they might go to someone else.'
- 'We can't wait for the credit rating, we might lose the order.'
- 'Unless you pay by next week, we will not supply you any more.'

Things that *ineffective* cash flow companies will do:

- Fail to be clear about payment terms at the outset.
- Encourage sales people to ignore cash collection.
- Regard cash collection as a minor function.
- Fail to give anyone clear responsibility for cash collection.
- Leave that phone call until tomorrow.
- Feel guilty about asking for money.

09 managing stock levels

In this chapter:
- types of stock
- key drivers of stock levels
- actions to minimize stock
- the cost of holding stock
- monitoring stock levels
- stocks of work-in-progress and finished goods
- stock comparisons

Types of stock

As with many questions around working capital, the nature of stock all depends upon the industry sector. Some businesses in the service sector require little or no investment in stock at all, because they provide a service rather than a tangible product – for instance a consultancy, an airline or a provider of computer software.

We should first of all define what we mean by stock in this context; *it is any money spent directly on products and services that have not yet been sold.* For a retailer or a trader the definition is simple: the stock is the merchandise that has been purchased and is awaiting sale, either in the warehouse or on the shelf of the store. For a manufacturing business stock can fall into three broad categories:

Raw materials

Amounts spent on materials or components that will eventually go into the product, but which have not yet been processed.

Work-in-progress

Amounts spent on products that are partly manufactured or processed but are not yet ready for sale.

Finished goods

Amounts spent on products that have been fully processed and are ready for sale, but have not yet been delivered to customers. Note that the definition from a cash flow point of view is the amount spent rather than the realizable sales value of stock, which also ties in with the prudent accounting approach to stock valuation.

A further category of stock that applies to all businesses is the amounts arising from other activities in the business: the stock of stationery in the various storerooms, the brochures that have not yet been handed out, the spare components for the office machines. In most cases these are relatively trivial and will not therefore be a main focus of this chapter; it is however worth thinking about these in the context of your own business – if you added them all together, how much cash is spent on such stocks and is it all really necessary? Have people in the business been ordering excessive quantities out of a misguided desire to reduce unit costs? As we will see later, this tendency to focus on cost per unit is one of the main causes of excess stock levels.

Key drivers of stock levels

We will focus first of all on raw material purchases or, in the case of retailers, the merchandise for resale. In all businesses, stock levels are mainly driven by human behaviour, choices made by those with responsibility for ordering supplies. Therefore the key question to ask when trying to ensure effectiveness is: are the people making these decisions aware of the financial, and in particular the cash flow, implications?

There is evidence that even major companies with specialist procurement departments are often found to be wanting in this respect so it is not surprising that cash flow does not feature highly in the thinking of those who have to answer the key question – what quantity should we buy? The factors that influence this decision usually drive towards higher than optimum stock levels, for instance:

Customer service

This is clearly a valid and praiseworthy reason for wanting to have high stock levels, particularly large quantities of finished goods ready for delivery. A marketing oriented company wants to be able to respond to customer needs as quickly as possible and having good quantities of stocks on hand may allow the business to do this more quickly. However, like all things in business, it can go too far. No business can have stocks in hand that enable management to respond immediately to any potential delivery request and reasonable customers will accept that. You have to make judgements about the most likely requests and match your stock levels accordingly. Remember also the story of Michael Dell of Dell Products who turned conventional wisdom on its head by realizing that customers were prepared to wait for a product that was truly tailored to their needs, thus eliminating the need for finished goods stocks.

Another point to bear in mind here is that customers will, wherever possible, want you to hold stock for them, because they have their own cash flow targets. Therefore you will need sometimes to be assertive when faced with requests to hold stocks of made-to-order products; there may be occasions when you have to accept this kind of request but not without an assessment of the pros and cons, and not without considering the financial implications – and therefore the price – when you are negotiating.

Minimizing unit costs

One of the main reasons for high stocks of raw materials, and sundry items like brochures and stationery, is the well-intentioned desire to minimize unit costs. This is but one example of the tendency of managers in businesses to regard cost as more important than cash flow, but it goes further than that. The suppliers of materials, ingredients, stationery and computer equipment are all likely to have one objective in common, the same objective as you have in your business; they will want to maximize their sales in the short term. There may be suppliers who take a longer-term view and only encourage you to take the right amount for you, but you should not depend on their having such a considerate and far sighted attitude.

Naturally one way of maximizing the order from the suppliers' point of view is to point out how your *cost per unit* will be reduced if you order more. This is particularly prevalent in industries like printing, where there is a bespoke product and the **marginal cost** of producing more brochures or packaging types is low compared to the total cost. It is vital to resist this argument and not to buy more than you know you need; the unit cost argument does not work if you never have to use the surplus, or if it takes several years before all the stock is required. And if it is several years before the material, component or brochure is to be used up, there is a strong chance that it will have become out of date or out of condition by then.

You should however bear in mind that often the requirement of suppliers to have minimum order quantities or prices linked to volume is quite reasonable from their point of view and is unlikely to change at your request, particularly if you are for them, a relatively small customer. Therefore there will be a case for shopping around and looking for a smaller scale supplier who will value your business more and will be prepared to supply in quantities that better suit your needs.

A desire for convenience

Another driver of high stock levels is the convenience of those who are running the business. It simplifies matters if you can have high levels of stock on hand and not have to keep going back to order more. It is easier to have everything on the premises and not to have to worry about stocks running out in the foreseeable future.

It is not suggested that such arguments should always be rejected but the cash flow implications, and the cash situation of your business, should always be considered by those who make buying decisions. One decision of this kind may not be significant but, collectively, such attitudes can have a major impact on cash flow and storage capacity. And it should be borne in mind that storage capacity will come through to impact cash flow if, at a later stage, further capital expenditure on new warehousing is required.

Complexity of product range

There are two natural desires of ambitious managers running any business – to *innovate* and to *expand*. These are desires to be encouraged and are usually positive for the business but there has to be a balance with the financial implications, particularly if the expansion of sales is to be achieved by launching many new product variations. This can be particularly relevant when you are producing tailored versions of products for particular customers, each of which will require its own special stockholding.

Every time the management of the business introduces a new version of a product, there will be implications for stock levels. There will probably be new types of raw material and packaging to buy and, in particular, increased levels of work-in-progress in the factory and finished goods stocks in the warehouse.

Actions to minimize stock

There are a number of measures that the cash flow conscious company should take to control stocks in the light of these pressures:

Education

The first requirement is to make sure that everyone in the business who orders supplies, or who is involved in the decision to buy, understands the need, from a financial point of view, to minimize stock levels. We are not necessarily talking about a detailed understanding of the economics of ordering – see later – but an awareness of the pressures mentioned above and the need, unless there are compelling arguments the other way, to keep stocks at the lowest possible level.

Authorization

It is also important that the major decisions around quantities to buy are taken at the appropriate level. The position in some businesses can sometimes be rather like the point made in the context of capital expenditure in Chapter 07; there is detailed spending control around relatively trivial amounts of cost but, because it does not immediately impact the P&L, amounts of cash that far exceed the expense budgets can be spent on, say, raw materials stocks without any formal authorization.

This is even more important where those involved in buying are encouraged – perhaps by the performance measurement system – to make apparent unit cost savings by buying large quantities, particularly if there is doubt about quantities to be required, or a danger of obsolescence. Those involved in the buying decision should be required to consult with someone at a higher level for any order above an agreed amount, which will be determined by the size and nature of the business. As with capital expenditure, £500 is a good guideline as a limit for the smaller business.

Challenging the options

Linked to this need for education and authorization, is the requirement to look at a range of options before major ordering decisions are made including, if possible without seriously impacting quality, the consideration of other potential suppliers. There is a tendency for arrangements with suppliers to become too cosy and though it is time consuming and uncomfortable to shop around and benchmark, it must be considered if existing suppliers are inflexible about size of orders.

Clearly this is likely to be more practical where the supplies are standard commodities available from a number of companies of equal standing and you are in a relatively strong buying position. It is also accepted that there will be many more reasons for shopping around other than order quantities. But the important message is that the buyer should not accept without question the supplier's preferences for order size and delivery time. Suppliers often have a habit of producing a few more options themselves when faced with an assertive customer who is prepared to go elsewhere.

The cost of holding stock

There are complex techniques for evaluation of economic batch quantities that go far beyond the scope of this book and which are unnecessary for the average small to medium sized business. It is however possible to make some relatively simple calculations, using a similar approach to the evaluation of credit terms to customers in Chapter 08. It is likely however that any simple estimate of the cost of holding stock will understate the true cost. Holding stock is not just about cash flow and interest costs – it is also about taking up space in the warehouse, the time of staff employed to handle it, and the potential losses through deterioration and obsolescence.

The pure financial cost of holding stock is relatively straightforward in comparison. The first stage in evaluation is to think in terms of number of days' usage. If your raw material is being consumed at the rate of £1,000 per week and you buy £4,000 worth of stock, this will be the equivalent of four weeks' usage. For simplicity we will call that one month's stock.

We will now make the same assumption about interest rates as we made when discussing debtors in Chapter 08; that the rate is 12% per year, or 1% per month.

We can now look at three options:

- One month's stock, 100 tonnes at £100 per tonne = £10,000
- Two months' stock, 200 tonnes at £99 per tonne = £19,800
- Six months' stock, 600 tonnes at £97 per tonne = £58,200

It should be pointed out that the cash flow implications of the three options are clear. The total money amounts will impact the cash flow and, whatever the cost savings, this is the first stage of the decision. It is critical that those making the decision look at the total amount, rather than being distracted from the cash reality by quotations of unit cost. Further considerations are, have we got the cash, is it within our forecast, what else could we do with the money?

The next stage is to increase each of the three cost quotations by 1% for each month during which stock is tied up, as follows:

	£
One month's stock, 100 tonnes at £100 per tonne =	10,000
Plus 1% interest	100
Total cost	10,100
Unit cost	101.00

	£
Two months' stock, 200 tonnes at £99 per tonne =	19,800
Plus 2% interest	396
Total cost	20,196
Unit cost	100.98

	£
Six months' stock, 600 tonnes at £97 per tonne =	58,200
Plus 6% interest	3,492
Total cost	61,692
Unit cost	102.82

The conclusion is that there is very little difference between the unit cost of the 100- and 200-tonne orders but the 600-tonne order is in fact more expensive per unit, if the interest cost is taken into account. And this would be even more so if the other extra costs of storage were added on. So, even if the six month order was within cash flow limits – highly unlikely if this is a major raw material component – it would not be justified anyway.

Monitoring stock levels

A critically important aspect of stock control is to keep a regular eye on stock levels and to have a system of reporting that is in line with the value involved. Clearly it is not cost-effective to have a complex tracking system and weekly stock takes for the stationery stock, but it is important that the major elements of stock are monitored and reported on regularly. In practice this should not involve much extra work, because stock checks are bound to be part of the management processes of those who decide when to order replacements. There should be a regular process of counting and reporting, using the above formula to express current levels in terms of days or weeks holding.

This type of control can be made even more effective if the reporting system is sufficiently well integrated to become the trigger for new ordering, so that it becomes well understood that replacement orders are not to be made until the minimum level has been reached, allowing a suitable buffer for contingencies.

Stocks of work-in-progress and finished goods

Work-in-progress at any one point of time is a fact of life for businesses that have long production processes, so the key decisions are those about quantities of finished goods which are made in the production process. The key principle is that those who plan production quantities must do so with the best possible forecast of customer demand, both in total and phased over the financial year, and must not be driven by a desire to minimize unit costs. Managers who are production oriented and are perhaps targeted to achieve the lowest possible manufacturing cost per unit, will often produce more than is necessary, because it is in line with their own key performance indicator. This is a classic example of 'silo' thinking and can be a key driver of excessive stock levels of finished goods and a cause of eventual write-offs.

The above is obviously only relevant to manufacturing businesses but there are some related issues around the equivalent of work-in-progress for project-based service businesses. In these cases the control and monitoring of *project work-in-progress* is critical to cash flow; for instance the major building contract, the software installation project, the consultancy assignment. The work-in-progress for these projects will represent the costs of labour and overhead that have not yet been invoiced to clients.

Such work-in-progress is an inevitable part of doing business in these sectors and the key requirement from a cash flow point of view is to have regular valuations and reviews, and to invoice in accordance with agreed payment terms as quickly as possible. It is surprising how many businesses of this kind are reluctant to ask for payments on account of work-in-progress, even when valued and certified, or to ask for stage payments. There is no reason why the supplier should bear the brunt of the financing of work-in-progress, unless it is clearly agreed otherwise.

Stock comparisons

We will finish this chapter by showing some comparisons of stock levels that illustrate two points:

- That stock levels vary because of the sector you are in.
- That this has enormous cash flow implications.

• That within the same sector, there will still be significant differences, based on strategy and product mix.

This comparison will show the sales and year-end stock levels of some major companies, and will then express these as a ratio of days held, for example:

	£
Sales	500,000
Stock at year end	50,000
Ratio in days = 50/500 (10%) × 365 = 36.5 days	

In practice this is not a pure measure of days held because stock is valued at cost whereas sales are at selling prices, but it will be valid enough for the comparison we are making. Also note that there are different currencies so it is the relative ratios rather than the numbers that are relevant:

Retail (millions)		Sales	Stock	Days held
Woolworths	(£)	2,737	377	50
Tesco	(£)	42,641	1,931	16
Wal-mart	($)	344,992	33,685	36

Clearly the differences in days held partly reflect the different ranges of products sold by these retailers and there are many other factors that would need to be taken into account before drawing any conclusions. But it should be realized that a company's product range is decided by the strategy of top management and can be changed; for example, Tesco's move into non-food products has brought their stock level up from around 11 days a decade ago to its current level of 16 days.

One interesting calculation arising from the above is that Wal-mart would generate $19 billion dollars cash flow if its management could bring their stocks down to Tesco's level!

Computer equipment ($ millions)	Sales	Stock	Days held
Dell	55,908	576	4
Hewlett-Packard	91,658	7,750	31
Canon	34,931	4,530	47

The differences between Dell and competitors will come as no surprise from the reading of earlier chapters – a stark confirmation of the impact of Dell's business model. If Hewlett-Packard could get down to Dell's stock level – assuming that they adopted the same business model – they would generate $6.8 billion cash for their shareholders!

Doesn't this chapter assume that stock is paid for in cash?

Yes, and this is deliberate, because we are dealing with the payment of creditors as a separate issue in the next chapter. At this stage it is enough to say that, if stock can be fully funded by creditors, the impact on cash flow is zero. For instance if Walmart were to take an average of 36 days credit from their suppliers, their *net* stockholding would be zero. This is why the management of creditors is such an important part of cash flow control and is the topic of the next chapter.

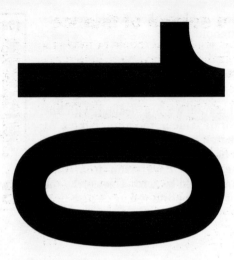

10

using supplier credit as a source of finance

Supplier credit as a source of finance

Assuming that supplier credit is available, it should be used as a source of finance, but with a number of reservations. Indeed you could go further and say that, unless there are special factors, taking credit from suppliers is not only acceptable, it is strongly advisable from a cash flow perspective and is, in normal circumstances, to be recommended as a business practice.

The reason for this is simple; supplier credit is effectively free finance for your business which is available from no other source. Every time you fail to take the maximum credit that is allowed by your suppliers, you are costing your business cash and profit, because you will be paying interest on borrowings that would otherwise not be necessary. Or if you are in the lucky position of having a cash surplus, you are forgoing interest that you could have received by delaying payments further and depositing your cash in the bank.

The simple calculation carried out for debtors and stock applies equally to creditors. If you are purchasing £10,000 per month raw materials and interest rates are 12% per year or 1% per month, the financial benefit to you of taking a month's credit is 1% of £10,000 or £100. Even more important if you are in a tight cash flow position, is the fact that you do not have to go to the bank to ask for that £10,000 and, by the time it has to be paid, money will have hopefully been received from your customers to improve your cash position. The longer you wait to pay your suppliers, the better your cash flow position will be and the less loan or shareholder finance you will have to obtain.

However, there are a number of reservations which make this a difficult choice, requiring balanced business judgement. We will look at each of these reservations in turn:

Long-term sustainability

One problem with treating supplier credit as a source of finance is that it is not something you can necessarily depend upon in the long term. If you take a long-term loan from the bank, you can assume that as long as you pay your interest on time, it will not have to be repaid until the due date, at which time – assuming that you are still creditworthy – you will probably be able to renew the loan.

In contrast, a supplier can suddenly decide at any time that it will no longer provide credit, maybe because of its own cash flow problems, or because of a change in policy or because they have doubts about your ability to pay. This may be regarded as unlikely and there may be other suppliers that are willing to step in, but it must be seen as a possibility. It is therefore vital to have a contingency plan to fill the gap – for instance an emergency cash fund or an extra overdraft limit – if the worse should happen. It is an important principle that you should not allow cash flow problems to be triggered by the actions of others that are outside your control.

Impact on creditworthiness

When new suppliers and credit-rating agencies assess a company's financial status, there are a number of key indicators that they look at to assess liquidity and solvency. They are naturally concerned about companies that take excessive credit from suppliers, because of the point made above – that such a source of finance may not be sustainable long term. This concern will be even greater if there are other sources of finance that might have to be repaid in the short term, for instance money owing for tax or a bank overdraft.

A standard measure of a company's ability to withstand pressure from short-term creditors is the **liquidity ratio** which is taken from the Balance Sheet and which looks at:

> Current assets – stock, debtors and cash
>
> As a ratio of
>
> Current liabilities – creditors, tax owing and overdraft

There may be some other sundry items in **current assets** and **current liabilities** but those shown above are the most important elements.

By calculating this ratio the analyst is saying, 'What if this company was asked to pay off all its current (short-term) liabilities, to what extent would it be able to do so from realisable assets?'

Though a lot will depend on the sector and the track record of the company, a 'rule of thumb' is that a secure company should have a liquidity ratio of 2, as calculated in this simple example:

```
Current assets    200 – stock (100) debtors (70) and cash (30)
                  ───
Current liabilities 100 – creditors (50) tax owing (30) and overdraft (20)

Liquidity ratio = 2
```

A second test, because stock is usually difficult to realize quickly, is to calculate the same ratio, but with stock excluded from current assets, often called the **quick ratio** or **acid test**. In this case the minimum is normally regarded as a ratio of 1.0, as follows:

```
Liquid assets     100 – debtors (70) and cash (30)
                  ───
Current liabilities 100 – creditors (50) tax owing (30) and overdraft (20)

Quick ratio = 1
```

The implications for a company that takes a high level of credit from its suppliers, is that these ratios will look low compared to others in the sector and will raise concerns about its ability to pay, unless there is a large amount of cash and debtors outstanding to provide a counterbalance.

Not only might a below-norm liquidity level make it difficult to obtain new lines of credit, it might also concern existing suppliers and lenders, causing the very thing that is dangerous to any business – doubts about the ability to pay debts if required to do so. The reality of taking credit is that there is usually no problem as long as confidence is maintained but, as soon as potential vulnerability is shown to the outside world, that essential confidence can be lost.

Hidden cost

It is an often quoted cliché of business that 'there is no such thing as a free lunch' and business people often argue that there is no such thing as free credit. The very fact that you can often get a discount for cash or quick payment – see later – often leads managers to think that they are, in the long run, paying more because they are taking credit from suppliers. The argument is that suppliers increase the price for all those who are taking normal credit, and even more to those who take longer to pay.

This can happen and should be watched carefully, but it is by no means the norm. The reality is that pricing decisions in most organizations are by no means as precise and focussed as that;

often those who set the prices do not know, and may not be responsible for, the cash received and therefore do not care too much about the time taken to pay. The two processes of pricing and monitoring credit are quite separate in most businesses and, unless there is a special initiative, these are unlikely to be closely connected. It can be argued that, in the long term, businesses will have to adjust their prices to pay for the interest and thus maintain their profits but, if that is the case, this will usually be borne by all customers, rather than those that take longer to pay.

Impact on supplier stability

The extent to which supplier stability should be a factor in your decision depends a lot on the size, reputation and financial stability of the supplier, and how much you need their continued support to maintain your competitive advantage. If your supplier is a small business that is struggling to survive and provides products and services that are critical to your business, it does not make sense to take credit in excess of what is reasonable and normal. And if you are in a stronger cash flow position than them, it may be best to pay them more quickly than the norm, to ensure their continued financial stability.

It is also arguable that such gestures can pay off in the long term, maybe at a future date when special support is required. Though it may be tempting to take advantage of relative power and pay as late as possible, there may be times in the future when the tables are turned, when there is maybe a shortage of supply and the supplier has products that are much sought after. Then the willingness to pay on time and be considerate to a struggling supplier may be paid back with interest.

One of the world's most successful retailers, Marks & Spencer, traditionally had a firm policy of paying all its suppliers within seven days, their argument being that this supported the many dedicated suppliers who were very dependent on M&S business, created mutually supportive relationships and reduced bureaucracy. This policy served them very well over the years and may have been a contributory factor to the excellent quality of their products and the high margins they made. The question that might be asked however is whether this policy should have been applied equally to large and small suppliers; it is questionable whether the much larger food and clothing manufacturers who supplied the company should also have been paid within seven days. Though it is difficult to know the latest situation without inside information, it seems that the 'pay everyone within seven days' policy is no longer operated so rigidly by the new M&S regime.

Cash discounts

Cash discounts should normally be taken, assuming that you have the cash available to make the required payment. It does however depend on the discount offered and the financial impact of the credit that you are foregoing by paying on time. As a rule of thumb a discount of 2% or more is likely to be worth taking but one under this level should be evaluated before a decision is taken.

The reason why 2% or more is likely to be worthwhile is quite simple: assuming a typical situation where a cash discount is dependent on payment within seven days and the normal period of payment is around a month, it is likely that you will be paying less than a month earlier than you otherwise would have done. Therefore you are getting a 2% price discount for bringing forward payment by a month, equivalent to a 24% per year rate of interest.

If the discount is 1% or thereabouts, the position will be less clear cut and a calculation based on the time period brought forward and the interest rate you are paying, will be necessary; this is the reverse calculation of the one shown in Chapter 08 when we considered debtors. However, there always has to be one important reservation – have we enough cash to pay within seven days? This may be particularly relevant when you are changing from taking significant credit to paying quickly; the change will have a 'one-off' impact on cash flow that you must be able to fund and maintain.

Delaying payment to help cash flow

Delaying payments to suppliers is common practice and the extent to which it is acceptable is largely a question of timescale and degree. Most businesses – and most individuals – have, at some time or other, held back cheques for a few days until cash comes in. This is part of sensible day-to-day cash management and the way in which you can avoid interest charges and, in some situations, bouncing cheques. But if this becomes a regular practice or involves holding back payments for significant periods, there is something wrong with your cash flow management and you are being unfair to your suppliers.

There have been well-known instances of major companies suddenly announcing to all suppliers that terms of credit will be lengthened, as a way of generating more cash flow. An example was Halfords who in 2003 moved to 90 days and in 2005 to 120 days. A lengthening of credit terms can be seen as a way of generating cash to support the financial structure of a private equity deal.

The cash flow benefit is clear; what is less easy to assess – and can only be decided in a long-term context – is the impact on supplier relationships, product quality and security of supply. There is also an ethical dimension that each company management must answer in terms of its own values; how far is it reasonable to suddenly change the terms of business without warning and what will this do to the reputation of the company concerned?

Should you choose a supplier because they offer long terms of credit?

It is certainly acceptable if, from other points of view, there is nothing to choose between suppliers. It is less advisable if, in other respects, the supplier concerned provides inferior products and service, though it is a matter of judgement how far these other issues outweigh the cash flow benefit. It will also depend on your own cash flow and borrowing position. At times of a cash flow crisis, terms of payment might have to be the deciding factor, though you should never intentionally allow your business to get into that situation.

You also have to consider why a particular supplier is prepared to offer more credit. When we discussed the opposite situation in Chapter 08, in the context of debtors, we warned about the dangers of attracting the wrong kind of customer. In this case there should be similar concerns and the question should be asked: why do they have to offer such an incentive? Is there something wrong with the product that makes it necessary to do this? You should also ask if this policy is likely to be continued or whether the terms will be reviewed once the supplier has attracted you away from competitors.

What about credit for major capital purchases?

In this case you should be negotiating credit terms with the supplier as part of the deal, and you should also link the timing of payment to your cash flow planning. In Chapter 05 we covered the importance of planning capital expenditure to coincide with the optimum timing from a *cash flow* point of view. This was assumed to be the time of purchase but it can be possible, by shrewd negotiation with the supplier, to have the benefit of the plant or equipment before the actual cash outlay.

This will of course depend upon your ability to negotiate such a deal and the impact on price. It will also depend upon your creditworthiness as seen by the supplier; it is likely that a 'one-off' supplier of a big ticket item will want some kind of credit check before allowing terms, as they are unlikely to know you as well as your more regular suppliers.

There are three points to remember in these circumstances:

- Make sure that you bring up the topic of credit terms early in your negotiations.
- Do all you can to take maximum advantage of the credit that is available.
- Match the timing of the payment to your cash flow plans.

What about payments by credit card?

This can be a preferred option for both parties. The benefit to the supplier – and to you if you decide to offer credit card terms to your customers – is that the sales will come through as for a cash sale, except that the amount will be reduced by the commission payable to the credit card company.

The extent of the benefit to you will depend upon the type of card, the payment terms attached to it, the time of the month you buy the item and whether you settle your account fully each month. You will not have to pay the amount involved until the next monthly credit card billing, which, depending on the terms of the card, could be almost two months away if the purchase is made just after the previous billing. You receive free credit without adversely impacting the cash flow of your supplier – a true 'win/win' situation, as long as the supplier is happy with the commission rate.

The benefit to you will be destroyed dramatically if you do not pay your credit card in line with the terms agreed, and start to incur interest charges. These are levied at an interest rate which far exceeds any amount that is likely to be charged by a bank and is a highly expensive way of funding your business. Only in the most desperate circumstances should it be considered.

Creditor policy

It is right to set a policy for creditor payment, but this will vary significantly between companies and countries; therefore any guidance that we provide has to be seen in this context. For instance, in the UK and many other countries, it is traditional for the wholesale meat markets to sell for cash or, at the most, demand seven day payment. In Italy, the norm for business-to-business dealings is for customers to take around three months' credit, unless there are unusual circumstances or special deals agreed. It is therefore important for those who are in charge of buying supplies of any kind, to know what is normal and to be aware of the implications of stepping outside the norm. In particular you should ask for price reductions when paying more quickly than the norm and expect – but maybe try to resist – pressure for price increases when taking longer to pay.

The sort of policy that might be agreed could be something like this:

- Take all cash discounts over 1%.
- Pay all major raw material suppliers within 30 days of invoice (or 30 days after the end of the month of invoicing, which allows more credit and enables all payments to be grouped together as one process).
- Pay all small local suppliers and selected others within seven days of invoice.
- Negotiate terms on major capital projects to achieve longest possible credit period.
- Pay sundry supplies on credit card where agreeable to the supplier.

In reality such policy statements might be varied informally by such pragmatic actions as:

- Pay the suppliers who are always chasing you for money as quickly as possible.
- Keep everybody waiting for a few days when cash is slow coming in from customers and (say) staff bonuses have to be paid.
- Delay payment to any supplier who is unpleasant over the phone!

Should you help cash flow by delaying tax payments?

This will normally be possible to some extent with all taxes and the extent of flexibility will vary by country, region and type of tax. There are three types of tax that are paid by companies:

- Tax deducted from staff salaries
- Sales/Value Added Taxes collected from customers
- Corporate tax on profits

In most countries, any delay beyond the required date for payment is likely to cause interest to be charged, followed by penalties/surcharges for the serious and regular offenders. In some cases however the interest charges are not high and it is possible to use delay as a useful cash flow lever from time to time. It is however important to know the extent to which delay can be applied and the consequences, so you should check with tax advisers about the pros and cons of delay.

It should be borne in mind however that, even when paid on time, the net impact of taxation on cash flow is a beneficial one. This is not significant in the case of tax deducted from salaries (which is paid over each month) but can be very significant in the case of VAT which (in the UK) is invoiced to and collected from customers, but is only paid to the tax authorities quarterly in arrears. The rules on corporate tax payment vary by country but are usually beneficial to cash flow; for instance a small company in the UK does not have to pay tax until nine months after the year in which the profit was made.

Creditor comparisons

We will finish this chapter by showing a similar comparison to the one in the previous chapter; in fact we will use the same companies. This will make the following points:

- That creditor levels vary between companies.
- That this has enormous cash flow implications.
- That it is interesting to relate creditor levels to stocks, to show the extent to which companies are using their suppliers to fund the stocks they have to hold.

This comparison will show the sales and year-end stock in days as in the last chapter, and will also show creditor levels on the same basis.

We confirm again that these ratios are not *pure* measures of days held because both stock and creditors relate more closely to cost, but the comparison is valid enough for our purpose and allows stock and creditors to be related to each other on a similar basis.

First let's look at the same retailers with creditors added as an extra column. Remember the way in which the days ratio is calculated, for example for Woolworths:

	£ millions
Sales	2,737
Creditors at year end	255
Ratio in days = 255/2737 (9.3%) × 365 = 34 days	

	Sales	Stock	Days stock	Creditors	Days creditors
Woolworths £	2,737	377	50	255	34
Tesco £	42,641	1,931	16	3,317	28
Wal-Mart $	344,992	33,685	36	28,090	30

As mentioned in the last chapter, the differences in days of stock partly reflect the different ranges of products sold by these retailers and this will also impact the comparison of days credit taken in relation to sales. Therefore our focus is going to be more on the relationship of stock to creditors, *the proportion of stocks held at the end of the period that are funded by creditors.* This is shown by the addition of two more columns to the table, as shown below:

	Stock	Days	Creditors	Days	Creditors to stock	Net stock days
Woolworths £	377	50	255	34	68%	16
Tesco £	1,931	16	3,317	28	175%	(12)
Wal-Mart $	33,685	36	28,090	30	83%	6

Note that the 'net stock days' column is showing the net amount of stock that has to be funded by the companies themselves. If stock and creditors at the year end are equal and the percentage of creditors to stock is 100%, this means that there is zero *net* stock to be funded, because creditors are funding it all. These are a few insights from the analysis:

- Woolworths appear to take the most credit from their suppliers in relation to sales, but this only funds 68% of their year-end stock, the other 32% having already been paid for.

- Tesco take lower credit in relation to sales but, in relation to stock held, Tesco are much better off. They have negative *net* stock because they have not yet paid for any of the 16 days stock held and there is a further 12 days unpaid for that has already been sold for cash by Tesco!
- Wal-Mart fund a higher proportion of their stock from creditors than Woolworths but less than Tesco; they have a *net* stock of only six days. However, if they could manage to create a zero net stock position by delaying payment for six days, it would increase their cash flow by $5.7 billion; if they could achieve the negative 12 days position of Tesco, it would generate cash of over $17 billion!

We can also look at a similar analysis of the computer equipment suppliers:

	Sales	Stock	Days	Creditors	Days	Creditors to stock	Net days
Dell	55,908	576	4	10,657	70	1750%	(66)
Hewlett-Packard	91,658	7,750	31	12,102	48	155%	(17)
Canon	34,931	4,530	47	4,143	43	91%	4

It seems that the computer industry is one where it is customary to take significant amounts of credit from suppliers, on average more than the retailers above. But the relationship to stockholding shows that the differences between companies are dramatic, in particular the extraordinary impact on cash flow of the Dell business model. Dell holds almost no stock but they have not yet paid for 66 days of the supplies that have already been converted into products and delivered to customers. Hewlett-Packard are also in the same negative net stock position, though nowhere near to the same extent as Dell. It looks as if in the computer sector, the big powerful operators are able to take long credit terms from their smaller and less powerful suppliers.

Canon – which is not such a powerful operator as the 'big two' and maybe adopts a different policy – takes less credit than its two larger competitors and does not quite fund its total stock by credit taken, only 91%.

We should mention again the other side of the policy of taking large amounts of credit from suppliers, which should not apply to companies of the standing of those mentioned here but may well apply to smaller companies. This other side is the question of what happens if credit is withdrawn. No doubt Dell would have the ability to replace their creditor finance with other suppliers or short-term loans from the bank but smaller less reputable companies might not be able to do so. The key question on the mind of every business taking credit from suppliers should be: what happens if it is withdrawn?

This is but one example of the point that has been made several times in this chapter – that the decisions around taking credit from suppliers are a question of judgement and balance. Taking credit will always help the cash flow in the short term but the key question is: what will it do to the long term and to the prospects of survival?

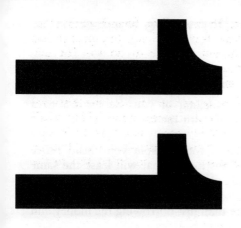

11

alternative routes to financing

In this chapter:

- an overview of alternative routes to financing
- factoring
- sale and leaseback
- financial leases
- operating leases
- guidance for choice

An overview of alternative routes to financing

The following options are open to a company that wants to go beyond conventional debt and equity sources:

- **Factoring** of debtors; the selling of your debtor list to a company that provides you with the cash, less a charge for this service.
- The selling off of assets – for example your head office building – to a financial institution that will lease the same asset back to you, usually called a **sale and leaseback** deal.
- Leasing of other fixed assets such as equipment and vehicles, under a deal that is more than just borrowing the money and contains other conditions and benefits.
- Leasing of the same assets under a deal that is purely borrowing under another name – known as a **financial lease**.
- Some other form of credit agreement that provides the same service as the purely financial lease, such as hire purchase or credit sale.

We will now look at each of these sources of funds, the benefits they provide and their potential disadvantages. Because the impact of the financial lease and the credit/hire purchase agreement are fundamentally the same, we will treat them as one for the purposes of this chapter.

Factoring

Factoring is potentially available to any organization that sells its products on credit. It can take a number of forms but essentially it involves the selling of the company's debtors to a specialist factoring organization – less the deduction of a 'factor's fee' – thereby converting the debtors into immediate cash. The impact on cash flow is very much like selling on credit card; you receive the money more or less immediately and there is therefore a positive impact on cash flow but you incur a cost for doing so. And whereas in the case of credit card sales customer pressure may give you no choice but to accept them, factoring is entirely at the management's discretion.

As with many situations around cash flow, the decision whether to factor depends on a number of issues and it is impossible to generalize, mainly because there are many types of factoring deals that vary widely in terms of cost and impact. However, despite the obvious and tempting cash flow benefit, factoring is generally seen as an expensive form of finance and one that is regarded by many as a last resort, only justified when other routes have been explored and ruled out.

What types of factoring deals are available and what determines the choice?

The first question to ask when considering this type of finance is: what benefits are you looking for? Do you just need cash flow upfront or are you looking also to reduce the risk of bad debts and/or take away the hassle of collecting the money?

If the need is purely for cash flow, the best solution is likely to be the least expensive option – a factoring service of the **recourse** type, where the risk of non-payment stays with the invoicing company. In other words, if the customer becomes a bad debt for any reason, the factoring company will claim the money back. If on the other hand you want the factoring company to cover the bad debt risk, you should look for what is the traditional and most common type of factoring, the *non-recourse* type, where the factoring company agrees to cover any bad debt losses.

It might be thought obvious that **non-recourse factoring** is preferable, but there are other issues to take into account. The first one naturally is cost; non-recourse factoring will be significantly more expensive as it is unreasonable to ask the factoring company to take the extra risk of bad debts without reward. The second point is that the non-recourse factoring company will normally be very selective about the types of debts which it will agree to finance, and will only want to factor the invoices that are almost certain to pay.

The other important issue to consider is how far you want your customers to know that you are factoring your invoices. Rightly or wrongly, factoring is often associated in some people's minds with a serious cash flow problem – 'they must be in a bad way if they're factoring' is what might be said. Therefore the other choice is whether to go for what is known as **notified factoring**, where the invoice states that the factoring company is involved and will collect the money. The other problem of this type of factoring is that you will be allowing another company to have contact with your customers, and that contact may not always be as gentle and tactful as your own approach; it will very likely fail to consider the importance of the future customer relationship. For this reason the alternative, the *confidential* or **non-notified** type of factoring, with the invoicing company retaining the responsibility for cash collection, is generally to be recommended.

It should now be apparent why factoring is often seen as a last resort. Depending on the choices made there can be adverse implications that go well beyond the financial impact and to this must be added the question of cost. The percentage charge range will be wide – anything between 2% and 10% – and this will depend on whether you choose the more expensive non-recourse and notified options, and the quality of the debtors involved. The extent to which the charges will be cost-effective will also depend upon the usual terms of credit and payment, but calculations in previous chapters have shown how the economics of cash discounts of even 2% are usually hard to justify on purely financial grounds and this will apply to factoring too.

The most common use of factoring is by new start-up companies that have to sell to customers on credit and have found it difficult to obtain enough finance for working capital from the more traditional sources of debt and equity mentioned in Chapter 06. The use of such a service may be tempting as a quick way to raise cash in the early stages of a fast growing but under-capitalized business, but any proposed deal should be carefully evaluated before a decision is made.

Sale and leaseback

This type of finance traditionally involves land and buildings but has now become available for other types of assets. The most commonly seen application involves the selling of existing land and buildings to a property company and leasing them back over a long period, the lease cost and timescale to be negotiated as part of the deal. The company receives the negotiated price in cash and commits to an agreed rent, which is likely to be reviewed at several intervening periods over the life of the lease. There may also be options to renew once the initial period has expired.

Whereas factoring is mostly chosen by the smaller business that is short of cash and unable to raise it from other sources, sale and leaseback is a method of financing that is more commonly used by larger businesses, including many leading blue chip companies. This is not to say that a smaller start-up company could not sell its property and lease it back; it is just that smaller start-up companies do not generally have valuable and debt-free properties to call upon.

There are three main arguments for sale and leaseback deals. The first is the strategic argument that a company involved in – say – the manufacturing of consumer products, is not in the property business, and does not therefore need to own its properties. There are other companies with greater expertise in this area and who will manage the property portfolio more effectively. There is no point in tying up potential cash and management time on an activity that is not central to the business strategy.

This argument is connected to the point made in earlier chapters – that a business should keep its capital intensity as low as possible to maximize cash flow. It is accepting that perhaps it was a mistake to buy property assets in the first place and sale and leaseback is a way to reverse that position, while still keeping the property for use in the business. It is interesting that companies with the largest investment in property – those involved in retailing – have different views about their strategy in this respect. Some buy most of their retail properties and actively manage their property portfolio; others choose to lease in the first place or go for a sale and leaseback deal at a later stage. Some may even combine the two strategies, for instance Tesco generally buy their properties but will use sale and leaseback selectively, selling and buying at what they judge as the right time from a property market point of view. This was reflected by news that Tesco, early in 2007, entered a property joint venture with British Land involving 21 of its new superstores, releasing more than £1 billion of capital and cash from its extensive stores portfolio. The deal was part of the strategy to free up £5 billion of capital by the end of the decade. The deal followed a similar exercise by J. Sainsbury, involving 127 of its supermarkets, realizing £3.55 billion, about half of the **book value** of its property assets.

Such large-scale sale and leaseback deals are not limited to supermarket groups; banking institutions have also been very active in this area. A striking example was seen in 2007 when a consortium of banks, including Santander and RBS, acquired ABN Amro. To enable the banks to fund the acquisition, Santander announced that it would be selling and leasing back its entire £4 billion Spanish property portfolio. At the same time

RBS was looking to sell a portfolio of properties with an estimated value of £800 million.

Are sale and leaseback deals usually driven by strategic factors?

There are many different reasons for sale and leaseback deals, and these are not always disclosed. Sometimes a strategic reason may be quoted by companies, even when their real reason is different – for instance that they are in urgent need of cash, or are tempted by the attractions of having it available. The reasons for wanting to realize the cash will vary for each sale and leaseback deal and might include for example:

- To reduce borrowing, maybe after an acquisition by another company or by private equity.
- To raise cash for an acquisition, or for a major programme of capital expenditure.
- To pay a special dividend to shareholders.
- To have a 'treasure chest' of cash for future opportunities and contingencies.

The other argument in favour of sale and leaseback is that the economics of the arrangement may be attractive, depending on the deal that can be negotiated. For a desirable property and a well-negotiated deal, the short-term economics can be highly beneficial to the seller, because the property company will be taking into account likely future capital growth; there may also be tax benefits, from the ability to set the lease cost against immediately taxable profits. A further benefit for the company keen to enhance its short-term profits, is that any profit on sale compared to book value can be realized and shown in the P&L which, under accounting rules, is not otherwise allowed.

For any business that has the unencumbered property assets to consider such a move, the above benefits must be set against the significant disadvantages of sale and leaseback. The main disadvantage is that you are losing the benefit of owning the property and, depending on the length of the lease and the detailed terms, giving up the flexibility of use and control in the future. You are also losing the financial flexibility that comes from owning assets that can either be sold or used as security for loans in the future. It is also true that, after a sale and leaseback deal, those assessing your creditworthiness will no longer have the confidence that comes from seeing valuable and realizable property on the Balance Sheet.

Each deal must therefore be evaluated on its merits; any company contemplating a sale and leaseback deal of this kind should get specialist advice and carry out a detailed evaluation – both financial and non-financial – before coming to a decision.

What other assets can be used for a sale and leaseback deal?

There has been a recent trend for finance companies to offer sale and leaseback deals on other assets; for instance a number of UK companies offer this service for owned vehicles, and IBM quote this as one of their financial services products for (IBM) computer equipment. Though some of the attractions quoted above also apply to sale and leaseback of these assets – particularly the cash flow benefit – it is much more difficult for the finance company to offer an attractive deal, as such assets are unlikely to increase in value in the same way as land and buildings. The question should also be asked: why not lease in the first place, rather than buying first and then leasing back? Such an arrangement could perhaps be justified if an asset has been bought for cash and then later the cash flow situation has changed, making it more necessary to gain the cash flow benefit of leasing. However, the economics and the attractiveness of the deal depend upon the valuation placed on the asset, the period agreed and the terms of the lease payments, which should be checked carefully compared to other financing options.

Financial leases

Before exploring the different types of asset leasing deals in detail, we should confirm the significance of the distinction between the two broad categories of lease. There are a number of types of leasing deals that are no more than another way of borrowing money, what we are calling *financial leases* (also the term adopted by the accounting bodies to describe a lease of this type). In practice, and leaving aside any legal and taxation niceties, a financial lease is no different from a hire purchase or credit sale agreement; it is just a way of buying a specific asset and paying for it in instalments, with interest charged at an agreed rate. The comments in this section therefore apply equally to hire purchase and other credit sale agreements.

Though there are some significant advantages to this type of deal, those involved should not fool themselves; the reality is that you are borrowing the money with just the same overall impact as if you obtained a loan from the bank, a situation that is recognized by the accounting rules. If a leasing agreement is classified as a financial lease, the asset goes into the Balance Sheet and the future lease payments are shown as a liability. In addition the interest payments are shown under that heading in the P&L. Thus an analyst who is assessing the ratio of debt to equity, or the extent to which interest is covered by profits, will not be misled by a financial lease.

The question therefore arises: why are financial leases so popular? Why do so many companies elect to sign leases of this kind on assets such as cars, computers, office equipment and, in some cases, plant and machinery? And why are there so many companies – often subsidiaries or associates of banks – offering this service? The answer is the self-contained nature of a leasing deal and its discrete association with a particular asset purchase. If you want to finance your fixed assets by raising long-term loan capital, of the type described in Chapter 06, you need to prepare a cash flow forecast which includes all your likely capital expenditure for a future period. You will then receive that loan in return for interest but there will be a complex loan agreement and the bank will probably need security of some kind. Between the time that you receive the loan and make the various capital investments, you will be holding the money and paying interest on it.

In the case of the financial lease (and the hire purchase agreement) the process is simpler and more effective from a cash flow point of view. You want to buy a car for £20,000; the leasing company pays the £20,000 and you only borrow that amount of money, paying instalments which combine capital and interest over an agreed period. The bank account is unaffected because the exact amount required has been funded separately at just the right time.

The major downside of such an arrangement is likely to be the interest cost. It is important for the person dealing with the leasing or hire purchase company to be aware of the potentially misleading interest percentages that are often quoted by sales people in this context. This is because the calculation is traditionally expressed as a percentage of the total initial cost at the time the asset is purchased, the £20,000 in the case of the above car. This is a flawed method of calculating interest because, *as payments are made, the balance owing reduces and will, over the life of the asset, average out at a figure that is less than the original cost. A useful rule of thumb is to assume that the average balance will be half the initial cost price.*

This means that the true interest cost is likely to be something like twice the percentage quoted, unless it is specifically stated that this is a genuine annual interest rate. When this adjustment is made leasing often turns out to be a relatively expensive form of finance, though its convenience and self-contained nature still make it an attractive option for the small business. It is also worth shopping around because this is a competitive market and, if your credit record is good, you may be able to land a deal that is cost as well as cash flow effective.

Operating leases

This term refers to any lease that provides more than a financial deal and is again the terminology that has been adopted by the accounting bodies. It may be defined by the offering company quite differently, for instance they may use the label 'contract hire' or 'equipment rental'.

An **operating lease** might include any combination of the following:

- An agreement to provide maintenance and repair services.
- A commitment to take the asset back at a particular value after an agreed period.
- An agreement to provide a replacement on similar terms.

In these circumstances it is impossible to separate out the cost of financing from the other aspects of the deal so the accounting treatment for the lessee is for the asset to be completely '**off Balance Sheet**' because the risks and rights of ownership are genuinely staying with the lessor. The only accounting entries required in the P&L are the lease costs, which means that anyone assessing the accounts of the lessee cannot easily know that the asset exists. It is only if they go into the notes of the accounts that they would see the future commitment to lease payments buried amongst the details.

The accounting treatment can indeed be one of the benefits of the operating lease, particularly for the company that already has a large amount of debt; it is a way of obtaining the use of assets without appearing to increase levels of borrowing. It also avoids showing large 'one-off' profits or losses on sale of assets in the P&L. It has an equal cash flow benefit to the financial lease without the inconvenience of having to admit the true debt position to the outside world. Whether this is a real and justified benefit is a matter of judgement and is dependent on the merits of each case.

On balance our recommendation is that the operating lease should only be taken out when the non-financial benefits are important and worthwhile. An operating lease should not be taken out purely to help cash flow, or to disguise the true debt situation in the Balance Sheet. There must be other benefits, for example the reassurance and cost-effectiveness of the maintenance or re-purchase guarantees. If these are not seen as true benefits you should go for long-term debt finance or the financial lease described above.

We should also make a general point about both types of lease that is often misunderstood. There is often a mistaken belief that a lease is automatically more flexible than purchase, because you are able to return the asset when it suits you and without penalty. This may be the case with certain types of operating lease but it is unusual, is likely to be expensive and will certainly not apply to a financial lease. It is important therefore to study the termination arrangements before signing any lease and to weigh the likely penalties against the probability of early termination. The reality is that, in most cases, you are more flexible if you buy, because you are then free to do what you like, when you like, with the asset concerned.

Guidance for choice

This is a summary of the features that are likely to guide the choice of financing source:

Factoring

- Last resort after other sources of finance have been tried.
- Need for cash early on in the life of a growing business.
- Relatively expensive compared to other forms of finance.
- Different types of arrangement, depending on needs.
- Often seen by others as a sign of cash flow problems.

Sale and leaseback

- Mainly for land and buildings.
- Typically used by large companies.
- Leaves property investment to the specialists.
- Keeps capital intensity low.
- Makes the Balance Sheet look less strong.
- Now available for other types of asset but not usually cost-effective.

Financial lease (and hire purchase)

- Another form of borrowing.
- Still shown as borrowing in the accounts.
- Relates to particular assets.
- Self-contained and discrete.
- Can be more expensive than it seems.

Operating lease

- Keeps assets off Balance Sheet.
- P&L impact more smooth and predictable.
- More than financial benefits.
- Can be more flexible on termination.
- Should be for more reasons than just cash flow.

12

formats for cash flow reporting

Cash flow reporting

One of the problems for those who have to analyse and interpret published accounts is that, over the years, there has been little consistency in terminology and structure. The P&L has had many different levels of profit with different terminology depending on the latest trend, and headings like 'exceptional and extraordinary items' have come and gone. The Balance Sheet has gone through periods when liabilities have been deducted from assets in a range of different and confusing ways, while some countries – notably the USA – have resolutely stuck to the traditional 'assets equals liabilities' format.

Unfortunately cash flow reporting has suffered a similar fate to the other two financial statements. There have been so many changes to the reporting structure and so many attempts to show every single detail that impacts cash, that the cash flow statement has become a highly complex and daunting document, which only the serious and experienced analysts are able fully to understand.

Cash flow statements began to appear in accounts during the 1950s in the USA, leading to the major accounting body, the USA Accounting Principles Board, first developing the *funds flow* approach to reporting in 1963. Prior to that time, cash flow was not reported as part of published accounts, mainly because there was no way of making it digestible and meaningful. A statement of the receipts and payments from the bank account is not helpful to management or shareholders, unless they can see how it relates to the running of the business, in particular the link to profitability. This was the breakthrough that the funds flow approach made, allowing the cash flow report to become the third key financial statement, supplementing the P&L and Balance Sheet with valuable insights for those who were able to understand and interpret.

The funds flow approach

The funds flow concept was introduced in Chapter 02, when we showed a simple example of a business in its first two years. We first showed cash flow as a statement of the bank account with all the receipts and payments as they actually happened – the cash collected from customers and the cash paid out to employees and suppliers. This showed a negative cash flow of £4,600 – in other words there was £4,600 less in the bank account than there had been at the beginning of the period.

We then showed how this same figure of £4,600 could be arrived at by the 'back door', by starting with profit and adjusting that profit for all the differences between profit and cash during the period. That, in simple terms, is what the funds flow approach is all about; it can also be called the 'sources and applications' method, or the 'indirect' route to cash flow.

This is the example from Chapter 02, showing this type of cash flow statement in its simplest form:

	£
Profit	1,150
Depreciation	250
Profit before depreciation	1,400
Increase in debtors	(5,000)
	(3,600)
Increase in stock	(1,000)
Cash flow	(4,600)

This simplified structure is the foundation for all the cash flow reporting that is seen in published accounts. It is based on the following logical process:

- Take the profit for the period.
- Adjust it for all the reasons for difference between profit and cash.
- Arrive at cash flow for the period.

To the example above should be added two operational items that would normally be present in a cash flow for a period – *any change in creditors and any capital expenditure*. For the purposes of this example we will assume that:

- Creditors have increased by £2,000.
- Capital expenditure was £3,000.

In these circumstances the above cash flow is as shown at the top of page 137.

Note that the increase in creditors is a positive cash flow, because it means that less money has to be paid out for purchases, whereas the capital expenditure has a negative impact, because it is an extra cash payment not previously reflected in the P&L.

		£
Profit		1,150
Depreciation		250
Profit before depreciation		1,400
Increase in debtors		(5,000)
		(3,600)
Increase in stock		(1,000)
		(4,600)
Increase in creditors		2,000
Capital expenditure		(3,000)
Cash flow		(5,600)

The above layout can be simplified by the clustering of the three working capital items – stocks, debtors, creditors – into one group, complete with subtotal, as follows:

		£
Profit		1,150
Depreciation		250
Profit before depreciation		1,400
Increase in debtors	(5,000)	
Increase in stock	(1,000)	
Increase in creditors	2,000	
Net increase in working capital		(4,000)
Capital expenditure		(3,000)
Cash flow		(5,600)

The clustering of the working capital items is useful to show the *net* impact of the working capital changes, and to confirm the relatively straightforward equation linking cash and profit, i.e:

> Profit, add back depreciation, plus or minus change in working capital, minus capital expenditure equals cash flow
>
> Or, in the above example:
>
> £1,150 + £250 – £4,000 – £3,000 = (£5,600)

This equation can be simplified even further if depreciation and capital expenditure are combined as one 'increase in net fixed assets' figure of £2,750 (£3,000 – £250). As we saw in Chapter

05 this makes the link between profit and cash easier to follow as below:

> Profit, plus or minus change in working capital, minus net increase in fixed assets equals cash flow
>
> Or, in the above example:
>
> £1,150 − £4,000 − £2,750 = (£5,600)

However this equation, though simpler, does not provide as much information for the analyst. As we will see later, the showing of depreciation and capital expenditure separately and the assessment of their relationship to each other, is important for analysis purposes.

Sources of information

It has to be admitted that arriving at a Cash Flow statement by the funds flow route is not easy and has challenged many an accountancy student during examinations. It is the task of a trained financial specialist, particularly when there are complexities beyond the above simplified structure.

We can however summarize the sources of the basic components of this type of Cash Flow statement, assuming that the analyst has available the other two accounting documents in their normally reported format:

- The operating profit figure comes from the P&L.
- The depreciation figure will be shown either as a cost heading within the P&L, or as a note to the accounts.
- The capital expenditure figure will either be shown in the Balance Sheet or as a note to the accounts.
- The working capital figures can be arrived at by taking the differences between the opening and closing figures in the Balance Sheet, the opening figures coming from the previous year's equivalent statement. For example, stocks £100 million 31 December last year, stocks £130 million 31 December this year, negative cash flow £30 million.

It may sometimes be difficult to reconcile the figures in published Cash Flow statements to the extractions above, because of the many complex adjustments that seem to be inevitable in big companies. But, in principle, the above sources of cash flow calculation should apply to all.

Formats seen in published accounts

What we have seen so far is not what is finally published for two reasons. First, because there are usually other adjustments that have to be made, for instance there might be asset disposals or changes in provisions. Second, this is only the *operational* aspects of cash flow; the complete statement should also show the non-operating items like interest, tax and dividends.

Therefore a complete statement, with some assumed figures for the non-operating items, might look like this:

	£	£
Operating profit		1,150
Depreciation		250
Profit before depreciation		1,400
Increase in debtors	(5,000)	
Increase in stock	(1,000)	
Increase in creditors	2,000	
Net increase in working capital		(4,000)
Cash flow from operating activities		**(2,600)**
Capital expenditure		(3,000)
Asset disposal		500
Cash flow from operating and investing activities		**(5,100)**
Interest paid		(300)
Tax paid		(400)
Dividend paid		(200)
Net cash flow		**(6,000)**

In the case of the 'below the line' items of interest, tax and dividend, the amount to be included would be the cash paid during that year, irrespective of the period it referred to. In practice it is very unlikely that a dividend would be paid to shareholders with the business being in such a negative cash flow position, but this item has been included for completeness.

Note that this more complete Cash Flow statement is now shown with two extra subtotals which are highlighted above at the levels of (£2,600) and (£5,100). As often happens with financial reporting, there is no consensus on terminology across different companies and countries; in practice both subtotals are often referred to as *Operating Cash Flow*.

How might these subtotals be used by analysts?

The level that we have termed 'cash flow from operating activities' – the calculation of which often appears as a separate statement or on a separate page in published accounts – shows the combined impact of the period's short-term operations, combining the generation of profit with the management of working capital, but before taking into account the investment and disposal of longer-term assets. If this shows as a negative figure, it means that the potential cash flow being generated by the business is more than cancelled out by the increase in working capital, which would clearly lead to questions about working capital management.

The lower subtotal – which we have termed 'cash flow from operating and investing activities' – is not specifically quoted in published accounts but is used as a key indicator by many companies for internal reporting purposes, highlighting the total cash generated from all operations, including investment in capital expenditure but before the non-operating, 'below the line' items. A negative figure here would indicate that the company is not generating enough cash to cover its investment needs, typical of a company that is growing and has plans for yet more growth. An analyst would study this level of cash flow in more detail, looking in particular at the relative impact and justification of working capital and capital investments.

Also important would be the comparison of depreciation with capital expenditure. If these two items are at about the same level, it means that the amount being invested in capital during this period is broadly the same as has been invested in the past, and the cash flow impact will be net zero or neutral. If capital expenditure is well in excess of depreciation as in the example above (£3,000 compared to £250) the net impact on cash flow is clearly negative and the analyst would hope to be convinced that this cash investment is related to substantial future growth and value creation.

Does such a Cash Flow statement always start from operating profit?

No, it always starts from profit but there can be different levels of profit, depending on convention and preference. Companies reporting under USA accounting regulations start their Cash Flow statements with the lower P&L profit level of net earnings for shareholders – that is after all costs and charges. This makes the statement shorter, as interest and tax do not have to be deducted, but it does mean an extra complication – that any changes in amounts of tax and interest owing have to be adjusted.

We will now make the challenging transition to a real-life cash flow report in this format. We will use as an example a grocery store with annual sales of about £350,000, making an annual profit after tax of about £12,000. Apart from a few sundry items being grouped together for simplicity, this report is exactly as it appears in the company's Annual Report. Note that this layout has a third section in addition to cash flow from operating and investing activities – *cash flow from financing activities*, in which are grouped the cash flow impact of changes in financial structure, and dividend payments. This is the company's published Cash Flow statement:

An example from a published report

Consolidated Statement of Cash Flows

	£	£
Cash flows from operating activities		
Earnings after tax		12,178
Depreciation		5,459
Profit before depreciation		17,637
Increase in debtors	(214)	
Increase in stock	(1,274)	
Increase in creditors	2,932	
Change in working capital		1,444
Other operating activities		1,083
Cash flow from operating activities		**20,164**
Cash flows from investing activities		
Payments for capital expenditure		(15,566)
Disposals of fixed assets		1,103
Cash flow from investing activities		**(14,463)**
Cash flows from financing activities		
Increase in long-term borrowing		1,441
Reduction of short-term debt		(1,193)
Payment of dividend		(4,990)
Cash flow from financing activities		**(4,742)**
Net Cash Flow (20,164 – 14,463 – 4,742)		**959**

The Cash Flow statement is then completed by the reconciliation of the net cash flow to the actual change in the bank account, as shown in the Balance Sheet, as follows:

	£
Cash and cash equivalents at beginning of the year	6,414
Cash and cash equivalents at end of the year	7,373
Net increase in cash and cash equivalents	**959**

Insights from analysis

This Cash Flow statement is showing how a company that made net **earnings** after tax of £12,178, only managed to generate £959 in cash, as confirmed by the opening and closing cash balances.

It is showing the cash flow picture in the following stages:

Stage one – operating activities analysis

- The earnings figure of £12,178 represents potential cash flow that would have been represented in cash if nothing else had changed.
- As depreciation is a book entry that has been deducted from that profit, this is added back and the potential cash flow is increased to £17,637.
- There is a favourable impact on cash flow from the company's management of working capital, because creditors have increased more than the total of debtors and stock combined; this is not unusual for a retailer that is growing and taking credit from its suppliers (this company's sales grew by 12% during this year).
- The combined impact of profit, working capital management and other operating activities, is that the company has generated £20,164 in cash which, if nothing else had changed, would have been cash in the bank; however, the investing and financing activities ensure that this is not the case.

Stage two – investing activities analysis

- Clearly the major outgoing of cash flow is the capital expenditure, which in this case is significantly more than depreciation and indicates a business that is investing in substantial improvement in facilities, or in extending its selling area. The management would therefore be looking for even more growth in the future, to ensure that this investment is justified.
- There have been some fixed asset disposals but this is not significant enough to have a big impact on the net investment figure.
- Investing activities take over 70% (£14,463 as % of £20,164) of the cash generated by operating activities, leaving the remainder to repay debt, pay a dividend or keep in cash.

Stage three – financing activities analysis

This stage shows what the management has done with the amount of cash that is left and how much will remain in cash form. It reveals the following insights:

- That the company has increased its long-term debt by £1,441, not too surprising or worrying for a company that is investing so heavily in new fixed assets.
- However most of that increase has gone towards reducing the short-term debt by £1,193, thus making the increase in total borrowing only £248 (which seems small in relation to the profits and to the amount invested in capital expenditure).
- The company has paid a dividend to shareholders of £4,990, which is a large proportion of the financing activities but which is just over 40% of the net earnings of £12,178. Earnings is the normal basis for dividend comparisons and this percentage is about average, though perhaps a little high for a company investing so heavily.

One further question that might arise from this analysis is whether the company needed to increase its cash balances by £959 and whether it needs to hold as much as £7,373 at the end of the year. We would need more information to answer this question but the general point should be made that there is no inherent virtue in holding cash and any that is not needed for future investment and for contingencies should, in normal circumstances, be returned to shareholders. This is particularly so for a retailer that has cash coming through the tills every day, though much will depend upon its reputation, credit rating and relationship with its bankers.

Free cash flow

Shareholder analysts will focus mainly on a level of cash flow that does not appear in most published Cash Flow statements, the *free cash flow*, the amount of cash available for shareholders.

This can be calculated by a slight but important adjustment to the cash flow above, which excludes the amounts distributed to shareholders, either by dividend or share buyback. See the worked example opposite.

This calculation shows the cash flow that has been generated for shareholders, after every other cash payment has been covered but before the distributions of dividends to them. It represents *their* cash flow for the period, both what has been distributed to them and what has been re-invested. If it is negative or significantly below the levels of previous periods without an obvious reason, shareholders would look for assurances that there are sound reasons that benefit the long term; otherwise they would have serious concerns about the lack of value being generated on their behalf.

The analysis of free cash flow by shareholders and their advisers goes well beyond the current year and is used as a way of projecting value for the future, becoming a major factor in determining share price. Analysts will justifiably argue that the long-term value of a business is ultimately determined by the future free cash flows it can generate for its shareholders and there is no point in buying a share unless its price is the same as, or less than, that future projection.

Cash flows from operating activities	£	£
Earnings after tax		12,178
Depreciation		5,459
Profit before depreciation		17,637
Increase in debtors	(214)	
Increase in stock	(1,274)	
Increase in creditors	2,932	
Change in working capital		1,444
Other operating activities		1,083
Cash flow from operating activities		**20,164**
Cash flows from investing activities		
Payments for capital expenditure		(15,566)
Disposals of fixed assets		1,103
Cash flow from investing activities		**(14,463)**
Cash flows from financing activities		
Increase in long-term borrowing		1,441
Reduction of short-term debt		(1,193)
Cash flow from (non-shareholder) financing activities		**248**
Free cash flow (20,164 – 14,463 + 248)		**5,949**

We will see in the final chapter exactly how these future free cash flow projections are used by analysts for valuation purposes and the absolute primacy of cash flow measurement as the determinant of long-term performance.

Would such a small business publish a cash flow of this kind?

No, because such a company is unlikely to be publicly quoted in the stock market. We must now admit a temporary deception in the interests of learning. The cash flow that we have just examined is not in fact a real-life example from a small retailer but one from a major retailer, the biggest in the world – Wal-Mart. The only difference is that instead of sales being around £350,000, these are in fact *around 350 billion dollars*! And, apart from a few simplifications to emphasize the key factors and avoid unnecessary complexity, this is how the Cash Flow statement of Wal-Mart appears in the company's 2007 annual report. The analysis shown above would also be very similar to the sort carried out by analysts who follow Wal-Mart and every other major company.

13

recruiting financial expertise

In this chapter:
- the range of expertise requirements
- different profiles of potential employees
- timing of recruitment
- the implications of business size
- a true story
- guidelines for employee choice

The range of expertise requirements

The ideal scenario, if cost was not an issue, would be for every business to have a qualified financial manager as an employee right from the beginning. But this is unlikely to be practical for the small business or the one working on very low profit margins, because financial expertise is expensive and, in any case, there would not be enough work for a full-time person during the early stages of most businesses.

Before thinking about recruitment, it is important to decide exactly what is meant by financial expertise and consider the various requirements separately. It will almost certainly not be possible to find all these skills in one person at the beginning, but it is useful to set down what a business, and particularly a new business, is likely to need.

The following expertise is required:

- The ability to talk to prospective investors and the bank manager about funding requirements, and the link to the business plan.
- The expertise to keep proper accounting records that will, if necessary, pass the scrutiny of an auditor; even if no formal audit is carried out, the records should be of the same standard, to protect from potential fraud and to satisfy the tax authorities.
- The production of the three financial statements that report performance and satisfy regulatory authorities – P&L, Cash Flow and Balance Sheet.
- The management of the cash flow on a day-to-day basis, receiving cash and paying bills, while keeping within financial limits.
- The ability to produce P&L and Cash Forecasts as described in Chapter 05, requiring a combination of accounting and spreadsheet expertise.
- The production of management accounting information to help decisions, e.g. product costs, comparisons against plan, debtor levels etc.

Can't this be done by the founders or other managers?

It is possible if the relevant people have accounting expertise. For instance, if there is someone with an accounting background in the management team, he or she would probably be able to do some or all of the above tasks. Otherwise it would be a tremendous risk with some serious potential consequences if it goes wrong. This applies particularly to the keeping of accounting records and the production of financial statements; this requires someone with financial training, who has acquired specialist skills over several years. The best possible guarantee of this is to find someone who is qualified with a reputable accounting body.

There is another argument against one of the founders or top management doing the accounting on a part-time basis. For most start-ups time is a limited resource and there are not enough hours in the day to do everything. Producing the accounts will be time-consuming, particularly if it has been some time since that person has carried out such work. It is best that their time should be focussed on the core business of the enterprise, not on a specialized accounting task that can be done by others.

Inevitably a new business will be limited by what is affordable, but this should only determine the type of employment arrangement that you fix and the hours that are worked, not the type of skills that you recruit. No business can afford *not* to have accounting expertise in one form or another.

Different profiles of potential employees

There are a number of options for recruitment of someone to keep accounting records and produce financial statements in the early stages. These are:

- A local accounting firm, probably the same firm that carries out the audit, though this will probably be an expensive option.
- A self-employed qualified accountant who specializes in helping a number of small businesses with this kind of work and would be able to attend on a regular but part-time basis.
- A part-time employee, perhaps an experienced accountant who wants to work part-time.

In the last two cases, it is important that the person is qualified and, unless you know them very well already, that the evidence of qualification is produced and verified. It is possible that someone unqualified could do the job but the risks are high, both of incorrect accounting and potential fraud. Anyone who has access to cash collections and the company cheque book must be subject to every possible check on personal history. This should not be confined to just checking the qualification; references should be taken and followed up.

Does the person have to fulfil all six of the above requirements?

Ideally yes, but this is unlikely to be found in one person. The best scenario is to find an individual who is financially qualified with a reputable accounting body and who has also worked in business; such a person will not only have produced accounts but will also have produced forecasts and management information. The only requirement such a person might lack is the experience of meeting with investors.

If so, it will be worth looking around for someone else to help with this more specialized need, on the relatively few occasions that it is required. And the importance of this role should not be understated; those who have seen the mixed quality of presentations in reality television programmes like *Dragon's Den* will know that immense damage can be done to a good business idea if the person presenting does not have complete command of the numbers and a confident, credible manner.

Timing of recruitment

It is very difficult to specify a particular stage when you should take on a full-time person because businesses will have different levels of complexity and profitability, depending on the sector and the way the business operates. A business selling to customers for cash and buying raw materials from a cash-and-carry will have much simpler processes than the business that buys and sells on credit. The best way of assessing when the time is right is to calculate the cost and time being spent on your part-time people and judge when these exceed the likely cost of a full-time person.

Our strong message is not to rush into such an appointment and to be prepared to wait until you find the right person. You have to be as sure as it is possible to be about the person's honesty because the temptation and opportunity for fraud in a small business is very high and cannot easily be reduced. And if the person you choose is performing well, you want to be able to retain them as long as possible. That means providing the necessary motivation and satisfaction in a job which will inevitably involve routine tasks that will not appeal to every qualified person.

One suggested approach for a relatively small business is to look for someone with the necessary qualifications and experience but who has other objectives in life than career advancement. Such a person will be more likely to settle for the lower salary that you are likely to be able to afford; maybe someone who is mid-career in an international company and wants to spend less time travelling in a less stressful job, or someone who wants to devote more time to the family, maybe someone who has particular interest in the type of business you are in. You must be convinced that he or she will find enough non-financial reward to stay with you, because it is highly risky and potentially damaging to any business for the main financial person to be changing regularly.

The implications of business size

Many of the same principles apply to larger businesses. The scandals at Enron, WorldCom and Parmalat – where accounting controls were poorly maintained – and the resultant regulations that were introduced, have made the recruitment of qualified people to the top financial positions even more important. In some circles the conventional wisdom was that an **MBA**, or someone who is good at public relations, would be better as Chief Financial Officer, rather than someone with a financial qualification. But the aftermath of Enron has changed the mindset completely; shareholders, bankers and analysts like to see qualified financial people at the top of the finance function, because it reassures them about the quality of the figures and the management of the cash flow.

In a bigger company it is easier to find the right balance of skills, because there will be several people in the finance function who can be selected for specialist skills – keeping the books, handling the cash, producing forecasts and management information. There is, as businesses grow in size, often a natural split between the **financial accounting** side, which manages the record keeping, cash handling and production of financial statements, and the **management accounting** side, which handles forecasting and management information. These two roles require different skills and mindsets, which should guide the choice of people as the business expands.

A true story

We will end this chapter with a true story of the development of a management consultancy business and the financial recruitment traumas it went through during its 20-year history. The business was formed in 1987 and is still thriving. Two of the three founding partners were qualified financial people so the obvious early decision was not to waste money on an accountant, but to do it all themselves.

This worked well for a few weeks but then the business began to develop even more quickly than expected, the pressure to respond to customers was very high and, in any case, this accounting stuff was all rather boring. The two founding partners had forgotten how time-consuming was the detail, and how long it was since they had been involved at that level. Cheques remained un-banked, bills remained unpaid, the bank account was allowed to go into the red, and the partners began to argue about who should sort it out.

The outcome was a decision to recruit a full-time financial manager. It was felt that they could not yet afford a qualified person so they advertised for someone non-qualified with book-keeping experience. The partners interviewed a charming lady who seemed to have the necessary experience and she was quickly taken on. The partners were much too busy to check her references or assess her technical skills but she seemed competent and the other people in the office liked her. It was agreed that the auditors would help her produce the financial statements once she had produced a trial balance.

Things went well until the time for the audit when the auditors revealed that the financial records were in such a mess that they could not produce financial statements. They had to go back over several months' bank statements and source documents to find out what had happened. It turned out that the lady's past experience had been in a big company accounts department and she had never had to keep a complete set of accounting records before. She complained that the partners had been too busy and too often out of the office to help her as she had expected. She agreed to leave with a sizeable pay-off.

The partners agreed that what was required was a qualified person, even if it cost a bit more. They advertised and had only one applicant – a Chartered Accountant with experience in business, looking for a less stressful job after being asked to leave a major company where he had been financial accountant. He seemed to lack the charm of the previous person and none of those who met him at interview liked him very much, but he was qualified and it was vital to get someone quickly; the temporary person hired from the auditors was proving to be expensive.

The new recruit lasted only six months. He was technically competent and the books were beautifully kept, but he upset everyone he came into contact with, lacking any kind of interpersonal skill. His chasing of cash upset customers, his terseness upset fellow office staff and his arrogance upset everyone. The partners realized why he had left his previous company and regretted once more not checking references. To avoid a walkout by staff and further upset to customers, they negotiated another sizeable pay-off.

This time they decided that the recruitment of a financial person was not something to be decided lightly or implemented quickly. They took their time and built up a description of the sort of person they needed and who would be attracted. They agreed that paying for a temporary person, while recruitment took place at the right pace, was a worthwhile investment. They drafted an advertisement that emphasized the potential benefits for the right person: the intellectual environment, the potential to develop the role to include IT and administration, the easy-going work environment and the potential for growth.

Many were interviewed and they began to think that the ideal person did not exist. But eventually he walked in and it was obvious that this was the match that they had been looking for. He was another Chartered Accountant, but with much better personal skills. Moreoever, he prefered a small business, liked the consultancy environment, valued the opportunity to work on IT related projects. He was not ambitious for vertical career advancement and was more interested in time with the family and social activities. This time references were taken out and followed up by telephone; it was obvious that this candidate was as risk free as anyone could possibly be, a popular and competent person wherever he had been.

He is still working for the company, now Financial Director providing high calibre financial reporting, a self-taught expert on IT, a major contributor to consultancy projects and a trusted member of the top team.

Guidelines for employee choice

The key lessons to be drawn from this story are:

- Time and energy must be devoted to recruitment.
- It must not be hurried.
- Accounting skills and experience are essential.
- So is personal chemistry with others inside and outside the business.
- You must be sure that you are providing the right level of job satisfaction to suit the person's needs.
- It is vital to persevere until you get it right.
- Once you get it right, you can relax!

14

using your bank effectively

In this chapter:
- factors determining your choice of bank
- levels of service to expect
- controlling the bank account
- changing banks
- summary of good and bad relationships

Factors determining your choice of bank

There will be many factors involved in your choice of bank and a lot depends on the strength of your position in two respects. Firstly the issue which keeps recurring time and time again as we discuss cash flow issues – how sound is your business case? If you have a strong proposition with clear competitive advantage, you will be in a position to make a choice; if your business prospects are poor, it will be a question of what you can get. Bankers will not be falling over themselves to provide banking services to a business that has no future.

The second factor will be the personal track record that the principals of the business bring to the party. Normally the starting point for a new business will be the existing bank of one or more of the founders; it should not be the determining factor but, assuming that there is a good relationship, it would normally be the first port of call. But if there is a history of excessive credit and failure to keep to agreed repayments and overdraft limits, you will be advised to start at a bank that does not have detailed information on your transgressions!

The final factor will be whether you are to ask your bank for loan capital as described in Chapter 06. If you have enough cash already or have decided to go elsewhere for finance, your choice will be dependent on the services and advice the bank can offer you, and your assessment of the likely relationship. But if you want to obtain loan capital or an overdraft facility, your choice will partly be driven by which bank will be willing to provide you with what you need. Though it would be nice if those starting a new business did not have to go cap in hand searching for loan capital and the required overdraft facility, this is the reality in many circumstances.

If however you are in a stronger position with good personal track records, a sound business case and permanent finance already secured, you can then make judgements about the kind of treatment and service you would like to receive and the bank that is most likely to provide it.

Levels of service to expect

Despite what the advertisements say, the tangible, routine services provided by the high street banks are much less differentiated than they used to be. Banking has become much more mechanized and commoditized so that the speed of processing transactions and the levels of interest rates are likely to be in the same range. The choice should therefore be based more upon special added value services that only some banks provide and the 'softer' factors, in particular whether you can establish a relationship that helps you to run your business more effectively.

There are a few tests to help you assess the potential relationship. The first test is whether you feel that the people you meet really understand the issues and the needs of a start-up company and smaller business. A number of the banks have specialist departments to provide small enterprises with advice and support, which is more likely to produce contacts of the right kind. It is also important that there is one person who is clearly established as the main contact, who will either deal with your requirements and concerns, or will act as a bridge to get you to the right person. If your access to the bank is only via the call centre or the person at the counter, you should be looking for a more personal relationship.

The second test is whether the people you deal with seem to want to know about your business, for instance whether anyone visits you at your workplace and shows genuine interest in your progress and your prospects. If your existing bank has not offered to do this and it is something that you would benefit from, you should consider whether you have made the right choice.

The third test is whether the discussions about your financing needs are informed, fair and balanced, and whether there is an element of pro-activity about the bank's approach. The old-fashioned banking mindset was to wait for customers to put forward their needs, which were then met with doubtful looks and reasons why it would be difficult to provide what was required. It was essential for cast iron security to be available before a loan could be granted. The main concern was around getting the loan repaid without too much care about the way the customer's business was developing.

The more modern approach to banking is driven by a different attitude, where you are clearly the customer and where the bank is trying its best, within its own constraints, to meet your needs. Their representatives should be proactive in suggesting particular types of loan or deposit account that fit your circumstances. They should be interested in your cash flow forecasts and should ask perceptive questions about your assumptions and your strategy. They should keep in touch on a regular basis and make you feel that there is mutual trust and openness, that the bank is working as a supportive partner to help you develop your business.

There are however two sides to the relationship issue. The bank that provides openness and trust to its customers has the right to expect the same in return. You should have no hidden agendas from your bank and should try never to provide any nasty surprises. The golden rule is always to see problems early and to flag them up with the bank as early as possible; if sales are down and this is likely to lead to an overdraft over the limit in a month or two's time, then this should be highlighted as early as possible, with a view to achieving a mutually acceptable solution.

If you do not see the prospect of such a relationship and you feel that you would benefit from it, you should be shopping around for a bank that is more customer oriented. Again however we should warn that the wisdom of shopping around always depends upon your current circumstances – in particular the state of your indebtedness – and the attractiveness of your account to another bank. If you are behind with loan repayments and suffering a decline in sales and profits, that is not a good time to shop around. But if you and your business are in a good state and the existing service is not right, you should certainly be looking elsewhere.

What sort of advice should be expected?

This depends a lot on your existing knowledge and experience, and the advice and support that is available to you elsewhere. Broadly speaking, such advice should be around anything to do with financial products and services. However, there has to be a caveat. In some key areas the bank's advice may not be entirely objective; there may be a tendency to make a recommendation to do business with an associate company, particularly if issues like pensions, insurance or investment are on the table. This does not mean that you should not ask for advice in these areas, just that you should realize that it may not be objective and that you should probably look at other options.

You might also benefit from using your bank contact as a sounding board for your thinking on more general business issues, for instance whether you should expand into new areas or target new customers; it is often useful to obtain an objective external view. Whether this will work for you depends upon your own needs and confidence and the extent to which you rate the bank people you deal with. The ability to advise in this way varies enormously between banks and individuals and you will have to make your own judgement about the likely benefits.

Another potential area of advice might be of the kind mentioned in Chapters 06 and 13, how to find part-time financial assistance, and how to make contacts with private equity financiers. The bank manager may also be a good route into networking activities, as banks are likely to have contacts with Chambers of Commerce and similar bodies, and to know of business networking events in the locality.

Controlling the bank account

Effective control of the bank account is a key factor in the banking relationship. However supportive and open the relationship, you will lose their trust and confidence if you regularly exceed the overdraft limit without warning.

The principles of control of the bank account in the small business are no different from those that individuals should follow in their personal financial dealings. It is always important to know the bank balance in the worst possible scenario, assuming that all cheques have been cleared and no further money received.

Ideally the company's financial accountant should record the cash paid into and out of the bank account in a cash account as the transactions take place. However, there will always be timing differences between the balance recorded in the business **cash account** and the amount shown in the bank statement.

There are the following reasons for timing differences:

- Entries of payments in the cash account that are not showing in the bank statement. These will typically be cheques that have been drawn by the business but have not yet cleared through the banking system.
- Entries of receipts in the cash account which have not yet shown in the bank statement. These will typically be cheques or cash received by the business that have not yet been paid into the banking system.
- Payments out of the bank account, not yet recorded in the cash account. These may include bank charges, standing orders and direct debits.

• Receipts into the bank not yet recorded in the cash account. These may consist of transfers between accounts or other income not yet entered.

The following example shows a business with differences between the bank statement and the cash account, together with a simplified reconciliation:

Cash Account

Receipts		£	Payments		£
2007			2007		
Dec 27	Total receipts brought forward from November	2,000	Dec 27	Total payments brought forward from November	1,600
Dec 29	J. West	60	Dec 28	J. Lloyd	105
Dec 31	M. Barclay	220	Dec 30	B. Coutts	15
			Dec 31	Balance of cash carried forward to January	560
Total		2,280	Total		2,280

Bank Statement

		Withdrawn £	Paid In £	Balance £
2007				
Dec 27	Balance brought forward from November			400
Dec 29	Cheque		60	460
Dec 30	J. Lloyd	105		355
Dec 30	Transfer from deposit account		70	425
Dec 31	Bank charges	20		405

Bank Reconciliation 31 December 2007

	£	£
Bank statement balance		405
Add receipt not yet shown	220	
Bank charges not yet recorded	20	
Total to add back		240
Less cheque not yet cleared	(15)	
Transfer from deposit account	(70)	
Total to deduct		(85)
Cash account balance		560

Nowadays the development of technology and the availability of on-line banking makes such reconciliations much more easy and immediate. It is therefore important that you are with a bank that provides you with an on-line service that allows you to go into the account at any time to check the balance. This should be combined with an accounting system that enables you to reconcile your cash account in the ways shown; software packages that do this are now widely available. The benefit of this on-line access is not just that you are aware of any potential overdraft beyond the limit; it is also to make sure that any excess funds are transferred into an interest-earning account. Some banks even offer the automatic transfer of any balance at the end of the day to a flexible interest-earning deposit account. This facility reduces the possibility of an accidental overdraft and prevents you from paying interest while money is elsewhere on deposit.

Another important factor in bank account control is the careful planning of cash flow, as described in Chapter 05. This will enable you, if necessary, to put more funds in place or re-plan your major outgoings so that potential cash flow problems are avoided. You should however bear in mind that even with the best short-term financial planning, you can never be sure of cash flow. That delayed cheque from your biggest customer can make a nonsense of the most careful cash forecast, and you must have contingency plans in place and be able to manage trade-offs on a day-to-day basis to keep the necessary level of control.

Changing banks

You should not hesitate to change your bank if you are dissatisfied with the service you are receiving. You should however only do so after a lot of thought and after doing everything you can to make the existing relationship work. You should think even more carefully before changing if your existing financial position is weak – for instance if you are taking advantage of a flexible and generous overdraft facility. Other banks may say that they will provide better services and they may well do so, but if they are less flexible around the issue that determines your survival, you may regret the change very quickly.

You should also be careful of change for its own sake, even if your financial position is strong. If you have a good track record at a bank at both personal and business levels, this will be a major factor if, in the future, you enter a more difficult period when your financial status is less strong. When you move to another bank you are starting afresh and will lose the credibility and confidence that comes from a good long-term banking relationship. The message therefore is only to change when you have tried every way of making the relationship work and have given the existing bank every chance to put things right.

It also depends on your reason for change. If you do find superior service and products – for instance, higher deposit account rates, on-line banking, automatic transfers and unsecured overdraft to a good level – these are sound reasons for change, as long as you are sure that the new bank will provide the better service after the change has been made. It has been known for banks to offer an impressive range of services to attract new customers but then to withdraw some of them later. If on the other hand your problem is the personal relationship with specific individuals, you should make a careful assessment of whether the new bank will provide something better. The person you meet may not be the person you have to work with over the long term and it may be better to try first to change the contact with your existing bank, rather than move the account.

It is not generally advisable or necessary to use more than one bank. There could be a case for choosing another bank for surplus cash if the deposit account rate is significantly better, but then you are losing the advantage of that money being available to counter any overdraft requirement. It is also likely that the extra cost and complexity of transfer will outweigh any interest saving. It is true that some major international companies work with many different banking organizations to cope with multiple needs and countries, but this should not apply to the smaller business. If you have to go to different banks to get the finance you need, there is probably something wrong with your financial arrangements. Robert Maxwell's company was famous for having more than 50 banks just before his downfall and the reasons were not to do with requiring better banking services!

Summary of good and bad relationships

Comments from your bank that might make you think about looking elsewhere may include:

- 'Dial 1 for business accounts, dial 2 for personal accounts etc.'
- 'This is not dealt with by my department, ring ....'
- 'This is the way we do things.'
- 'Head Office don't allow us to ...'
- 'We have no product of that kind.'
- 'There is no way we can ever make a loan without tangible assets as security.'

Comments from your bank that should reassure you that you have got it right include:

- 'This is my direct line/mobile number if you have any problem any time.'
- 'We have specialists who deal with that requirement and I will arrange for someone to contact you within 24 hours.'
- 'Can I come to see you?'
- 'We have this specialist facility for small businesses.'
- 'What are the assumptions behind your cash forecast?'
- 'Have you considered what might happen if ...?'
- 'What is your competitive advantage?'
- 'What is your policy on giving credit to customers and cash collections?'

Things that you should be saying to your bank include:

- 'These are our plans for development of our business.'
- 'We expect a temporary cash flow deficit in two months' time.'

- 'This is the worst possible scenario.'
- 'I would like your advice on ...'

and if necessary:

- 'Unless the levels of service improve, we will be looking at other options.'

Things that you should *not* be saying to your bank include:

- 'There are not enough funds to clear the cheques we drew yesterday, can you allow/extend the overdraft?'
- 'I am not sure what the overdraft needs will be.'
- 'I should have told you about ...'

'cash is king!'

In this chapter:
- why cash is king
- cash flow and business valuation
- the implications for the smaller business
- potential business sale scenarios

Why 'cash is king'

There are a number of senses in which this phrase has been used in recent years. In Chapter 11 we mentioned that the main driver has been some concern, and even some disillusionment, with conventional accounting measurement, reinforced by the various accounting scandals, of which Enron was the first and highest profile example.

Even before these scandals brought things to a head, the more perceptive analysts had begun to carry out new and more sophisticated analyses of cash flow, moving away from conventional P&L and Balance Sheet ratios. They realized that the key difference between cash flow and the other two financial statements is that cash flow is not subject to accounting judgement; it has to be reconciled back to the difference between opening and closing cash balances which, short of outright fraud, cannot be manipulated. (Though it is interesting that the major accounting scandal to hit Europe – the Italian company Parmalat – did involve the creation of fictitious cash balances.)

In the fallout from the Enron affair, there were many 'wise after the event' commentators who remarked that, if analysts had focussed on trends in cash flow generation rather than in reported earnings, the true business position would have been more evident. This is easy to say now but was much more difficult to detect in practice, because the business operations and financial structure of Enron were so complex; indeed some might say that the complexity was deliberately increased by a management that was anxious to erect smokescreens.

The analysts' interest in cash flow statements has two main dimensions. First there is the sort of analysis we saw in Chapter 12, an assessment of the links between profit and cash, to assess management of working capital, fixed assets and the company's financial structure. The second element will be the main focus of this chapter, the use of cash flow projections to determine the value of a business, both for large publicly quoted and smaller unquoted companies.

Cash flow and business valuation

Cash flows not only impact business valuation, they are, in the end, the only way in which the real value of a business can be determined. Some might argue that the only true way of arriving at the value of a *publicly quoted* company is the stock market valuation but it is cash flow estimates that are behind such valuations, either by specific calculation or by the intuitive judgement of actual or potential shareholders. Any shareholder, large or small, must be investing to achieve potential future cash flows from dividends and/or from future expected growth in the value of the shares. Therefore every share purchase or sale – for that is what drives market prices – is based on the individual cash flow forecasts of each buyer and seller.

The same principle applies to business valuations that are made by the buyers and sellers involved in major acquisition deals. There will be other methods of valuation that are used in negotiations – for instance multiples of sales or earnings as shown below – but any well-run company that is making an acquisition will underpin its discussions with a forecast of the cash flows that it can deliver from having that company as part of its operations. The buying company should not buy for more than its estimate of the present value of the future cash flows that it will receive as a result of ownership; and the selling company should not sell for less than the present value of the cash flows that it will receive from retaining the business in its present form. And if these two numbers do not match, there is no deal, unless there are non-financial reasons for the transaction to take place.

All this is based on the assumption that it is possible to make accurate estimates of future cash flows and one limitation of this method of business valuation is that the outcomes are difficult to predict, particularly when one company is being merged into another. This is often the reason why deals are done; the buyer maybe has an over-optimistic view of what can be done with the business, or the seller does not realize its full potential, and these factors are reflected in their different cash flow projections.

The implications for the smaller business

The implications for the smaller business depend on whether sale to a third party is part of the future plans of those who own the business. If this is not the case, there is no point in projecting future cash flows to arrive at a valuation, unless there is a desire to know a likely price, should a sale become an option later. There is also an argument that minds might be changed by a valuation – everyone has their price – and that, in any case, owners should be prepared, just in case an unsolicited bid should come along.

If sale of the business is an option, future cash flows are the key to deciding when to sell and the price you can ask. In terms of timing, it is best to sell your business before any major outlay on capital expenditure, because you are unlikely to recover the cost of capital investment in the sale price. It may be a factor – particularly if the buyer will have to invest a similar amount – but this may not be the case.

The main relevance of cash flow to business sale negotiations is that future cash forecasts provide guidance in determining the minimum price that you should be prepared to sell your business for – your 'walk-away' valuation. This is not something to be shown to a potential buyer, or that potential buyers – armed with their own specific cash flow forecasts – will expect you to reveal. Open discussions are more likely to be based on multiples of sales or earnings, for example:

- 'For your type of business, the market price is ten times latest earnings.'
- 'We never pay more than half a year's sales for a company in your sector.'
- 'The last four deals done in your sector have been completed at around six times operating profit.'

Those involved in such negotiations will usually choose the variable that best suits the price they want to pay; if profits are high the buyer will probably quote a multiple of sales, whereas the seller will quote a multiple of profit. This is normal commercial behaviour and is to be expected. Those negotiating a business sale will not be open about their own cash flow calculations but these are likely to drive their negotiating behaviour.

Sellers should therefore make their own forecasts of the cash flows that the ongoing business will generate for the foreseeable future – say ten years – assuming realistic achievement of growth and profit levels. This should be supplemented by a forecast of what the business will be worth at the end of that period, either via a sale at that time, or as an ongoing business. These forecasts should then, with the help of a specialist financial adviser, be converted into their *present value*, using the techniques described in Chapter 07 and covered in more detail in the Appendix on page 171.

Potential business sale scenarios

Let's now illustrate the relevance of this present value calculation to sale negotiations with an example:

Janet and John revisited

Janet and John have been in business for five years. They have been approached by a major food company who want to buy their business. The key financials for the last year are:

	£000
Sales	2,200
Operating profit	200
Tax	60
Earnings after tax	140

The bidder has offered £1,400,000, justified by being ten times after-tax earnings. Janet and John's adviser has checked the market and it seems that the three quotations above represent the current market position; thus £1,400,000 seems a fair and attractive bid – half a year's sales would be £1,100,000 and six times operating profit would be £1,200,000.

Therefore, should Janet and John accept the £1,400,000 bid?

We can answer this question by assuming three different scenarios and present value calculations (capital gains tax is ignored for simplicity):

First scenario

The Net Present Value of the cash flow forecast for Janet and John continuing to run the business is £1,000,000.

Likely decision: Accept the £1,400,000 bid with open arms as it far exceeds the value that can be generated from the business by keeping it. Janet and John could still try to negotiate for a higher offer but without much confidence that it will be forthcoming. It would seem that the bidder has ways of creating value from the business that are not open to Janet and John – which might give them food for thought – or is making over-optimistic assumptions.

Second scenario

The Net Present Value of the cash flow forecast for Janet and John continuing to run the business is £1,600,000.

Likely decision: Reject the bid as more value can be created by keeping the business. Alternatively, try to negotiate the buyer up to £1,600,000, knowing that this is the minimum 'walk-away' figure.

Third scenario

The Net Present Value of the cash flow forecast for Janet and John continuing to run the business is £1,400,000.

Likely decision: Look at the possibilities for negotiating upwards but, if this is not possible, make a balanced judgement, based on personal preferences and risk factors. This judgement can be made in the knowledge that the bid is fair and is roughly equivalent to the value that would be generated by continued ownership of the business. A key factor might be the fact that the £1,400,000 from the sale is certain and risk free, whereas the future cash flow projections are likely to be subject to many uncertainties.

In the end, the decision might come down to what Janet and John really want to do and a key issue would be whether they are expected to continue to run the business for the new owners. This judgement clearly goes even further beyond the purely financial aspects of the deal, but these scenarios show how future cash flow evaluations provide valuable guidance to those who have to make the final decision.

So is cash king?

Yes, because whatever the Balance Sheet or P&L might say about current performance and asset values, in the long-term a business can only be worth the cash flows that it will generate in the future. If Janet and John do sell out for £1,400,000 this will be value for them, but the new owner of the business will only make the business worth what has been paid if the assumed cash flows are actually delivered. Similarly, the public company with good current profits, well publicized growth prospects and a high share price, will only deliver long-term value to its shareholders if the assumed future cash flow forecasts eventually materialize.

Cash flow is the only reality in the long-term life of a business. This is why 'cash is king'!

appendix

An explanation of the techniques of Discounted Cash Flow (DCF)

What is the total scope of DCF?

DCF (Discounted Cash Flow) covers all those techniques of investment appraisal that use the concept of present value. This includes NPV (Net Present Value), **Discounted Payback** and Internal Rate of Return.

So what is the concept of present value?

It is the conversion of money values projected into the future, back into their equivalent value now. As the financial evaluation of investments always requires projections of future values to assess viability, this makes the concept particularly relevant to their evaluation.

What is the starting point?

The starting point is the establishment of a **discount rate**, which is an essential first stage for the conversion of future cash flows into their **present value**. This is based on the company's cost of capital, the average rate of return it has to pay to obtain funds from its investors, both debt and equity.

So how does present value work?

Let's simplify at this stage by taking 10% as the **cost of capital** figure we are assuming and applying it to a personal situation. Assume that it is costing you as an individual 10% to obtain money from the bank or, if you have surplus funds, that you could obtain 10% by investing elsewhere. Also assume that someone is offering you the following: £100 *payable to you in one year's time.*

The concept of present value tells you what that £100 in 'Year 1' is worth today.

Would that be £110?

No, that is applying the technique of compounding rather than discounting, compounding projects future values from money today. We are trying to do the reverse, to discount a future value back to what it is worth today.

Would it be £90?

Not quite, but this is much closer and using the right approach. However, if you had £90 today and invested it at 10% it would not quite make £100.

$$
\begin{array}{r}
£ \\
90 \\
\underline{9} \ (10\%) \\
99
\end{array}
$$

So you would be worse off if you accepted £90 today, rather than taking the £100 in a year's time. The correct answer is £91 or £90.91 to be more precise. To confirm this we can do a similar calculation:

$$
\begin{array}{r}
£ \\
90.91 \\
\underline{9.09} \ (10\%) \\
100.00
\end{array}
$$

Therefore the present value of £100 in one year's time is £90.91 and the present value of £1 in a year's time is £0.9091.

Is there a formula for calculating this?

Yes, and it can be expressed in a number of ways. Those who know and like algebra would call the formula 1/1+r and those who prefer fractions would express it as 100/110 or 1/1.1. In practice however it is not necessary to work it out because discount tables are available with most conceivable rates and timescales and the formulae are also built into calculators and spreadsheets.

Can you take it beyond one year?

Yes. Let's now think about £1. Assume that you have been offered this amount in two or three years' time. We know that the value in one year's time is £0.9091. The present value can be calculated by continuing this discount process further, as follows:

Today	1.0000
Year 1	0.9091 (1.0000 × 1/1.1)
Year 2	0.8264 (.9091 × 1/1.1)
Year 3	0.7513 (.8264 × 1/1.1)

Thus we continue the discounting process into the second and third years, to find out the value of that future amount in today's terms. You can now say that, if someone has offered you £100 in three years' time and your cost or opportunity cost of capital is 10%, you would do just as well to accept £75.13 today.

But how does this help us to appraise investments?

It is extremely helpful in a number of ways. Let's take a simple investment project as an example:

Year	£	
0	(10,000)	(including investment)
1	1,000	(savings)
2	2,000	(savings)
3	3,000	(savings)
4	4,000	(savings)
5	5,000	(savings)
Total	5,000	

One of the problems of assessing the viability of this investment is that you are not comparing like with like. You are trying to find out whether it is worth investing £10,000 in today's terms but you are trying to compare it with values which are several years ahead. Also the values in the future years are not comparable; £5,000 in Year 5 is probably worth more than £4,000 in Year 4 but it is not valid to compare them without making some adjustment for the impact of time on value.

So how do we use the present value concept in practice?

By discounting the cash flow and converting it into its Net Present Value or NPV. Let's see how this works on our cash flow:

Year	£	
0	(10,000)	(including investment)
1	1,000	(savings)
2	2,000	(savings)
3	3,000	(savings)
4	4,000	(savings)
5	5,000	(savings)
Total	5,000	

The £10,000 is clearly in today's terms so there is no need to convert this to its present value but we must do that with the rest of the cash flow, as follows:

Year	£				£
1	1,000	×	0.9091	=	909
2	2,000	×	0.8264	=	1,653
3	3,000	×	0.7513	=	2,254
4	4,000	×	0.6830	=	2,732
5	5,000	×	0.6209	=	3,104

So what do we do now that we have discounted each year's cash flow?

We add them up to find out how the total of the present values above compares with the initial investment of £10,000.

Year	£				£
1	1,000	×	0.9091	=	909
2	2,000	×	0.8264	=	1,653
3	3,000	×	0.7513	=	2,254
4	4,000	×	0.6830	=	2,732
5	5,000	×	0.6209	=	3,104
Total Present Value					10,652

Is this total of £10,652 the net present value or NPV?

No, it is the present value of all the cash flows coming back; the NET Present Value is the total of these, less the initial investment of £10,000 i.e:

	£
Present value of cash inflows	10,652
Initial investment	10,000
Net Present Value (NPV)	652

What is this measure saying about the project?

First of all it is important to remember that this present value is after discounting at a rate which equates to the company's cost of capital, and which therefore covers the return required by shareholders. Therefore the NPV measure is saying that this project is viable because it has returned the £10,000 investment and has created £652 extra value on top of that.

So what is the role of NPV in the assessment of projects?

It is really the first hurdle that shows whether the project has made the minimum required return and how much further value has been created beyond that. If a project has a negative NPV (say in this case there had only been £9,000 positive present values and therefore a – £1,000 NPV) the evaluation is saying that this is not a viable project, as the initial investment has not been recovered in real terms. Therefore, unless there are very good strategic reasons or unless it is possible to improve the future cash flow projections, the project should be rejected.

So it really only provides a 'yes/no' decision?

It provides more than that. It shows you the amount of value created, which may be useful to compare with other options and to assess what would happen if assumptions were to be changed.

How would you compare with other options?

Let's look at a possible second project, which is seen as an alternative to the one we have been considering:

	£
Investment	(10,000)
1	5,000
2	4,000
3	2,000
4	2,000
5	1,000
Total	4,000

Note that the total cash flow before discounting is less than the previous project (£14,000 coming back compared to £15,000, thus the net cash flow is £4,000 rather than £5,000) but the pattern of cash flows is different. The £5,000 in Year 1 for this project is clearly worth more than the £5,000 in Year 5 from the earlier one and this must be reflected in any comparative appraisal. This illustrates the need for discounting even more clearly; any straight cash flow comparison would ignore this important difference.

So is it valid to work out the NPV of two projects and compare them on that basis?

It is valid where they are alternatives which you need to choose between, particularly where, as in this case, the initial investment is the same. Where these two circumstances do not apply, other methods may be better suited to comparison of alternatives but it is useful to make the comparison in this case for illustrative purposes. Let's discount this project at the same 10% cost of capital:

	£			£
Investment	(10,000)	×	1.000	(10,000)
1	5,000	×	0.9091	4,545
2	4,000	×	0.8264	3,306
3	2,000	×	0.7513	1,503
4	2,000	×	0.6830	1,366
5	1,000	×	0.6209	621
NPV				1,341

Why has this project ended up with a higher NPV than the previous one, when the total cash flow was lower?

This is the impact of discounting. This new project has its best years early on and therefore gets more value from the discounting process. Note the present value of £4,545 in Year 1 and how much more this is than the value of 5,000 in Year 5 for the first project of £3,104 (£5,000 × 0.6209).

So if you had to choose between these two projects it is valid to say that the second one should be chosen?

Yes, because it is creating more value. This is on the assumption that they are mutually exclusive and that you have to choose between them. Otherwise you should accept them both because they both create value. However, decisions about projects will usually go beyond financial measures and management judgement, particularly about the strategic implications, could be an even more important factor in the decision.

What other DCF measures are there?

A popular and useful measure is Discounted Payback. This takes the concept of payback and applies it in such a way that it removes one of its main limitations – that it does not provide a payback in real or present value terms. Discounted Payback overcomes this limitation by doing just that. For example, for Project 2 it would be calculated like this:

Year		Discount factor	Present value	Cumulative NPV
	£		£	£
0	(10,000)		(10,000)	(10,000)
1	5,000	0.9091	4,545	(5,455)
2	4,000	0.8264	3,306	(2,149)
3	2,000	0.7513	1,503	(646)
4	2,000	0.6830	1,366	720
5	1,000	0.6209	621	1,341

The cumulative NPV for the first three years shows the amount still to be paid back, by deducting the positive NPVs generated so far from the initial investment. Thus, at the end of the third year, £646 still has to be repaid, £4,545 + £3,306 + £1,503 = £9,354, having been generated in present value terms.

So what is the Discounted Payback Period?

It will be somewhere between three and four years, approximately half way. This can be calculated proportionally, assuming an even flow during the fourth year, ie:

$$\text{To be repaid} \quad \frac{£\ 646}{1,366} = 0.47$$
$$\text{Year 4 NPV}$$

Therefore the Discounted Payback is 3.47 years though to avoid spurious accuracy, a rounding to 3.50 would be sensible.

What is the place of Discounted Payback in the portfolio of measures?

Discounted Payback is usually the next stage of analysis after NPV has established a project's basic financial viability, to get a feel for the time it will take to recoup the original investment before moving on to assess risk factors in more depth. Clearly the longer it takes to pay back the more the risk exposure, because more things can go wrong and more assumptions can prove invalid as the environment changes over time.

The third measure mentioned earlier – Internal Rate of Return or IRR – how does that work?

The Internal Rate of Return is a method of calculating the break-even rate, the discount rate at which the project will exactly break-even, causing the NPV to be zero.

Why is it called 'internal'?

This is uncertain and goes back into history; it is not a very helpful or meaningful name and it would be better if it was called something else more descriptive, for instance 'break-even rate' would be a much better label.

How is it calculated?

Let's take Project 2 again and remind ourselves of the NPV calculation at 10% discount rate:

	£			£
Investment	(10,000)	×	1.0000	(10,000)
1	5,000	×	0.9091	4,545
2	4,000	×	0.8264	3,306
3	2,000	×	0.7513	1,503
4	2,000	×	0.6830	1,366
5	1,000	×	0.6209	621
NPV				1,341

We will now look at the impact of changing the discount rate by calculating the NPV of the same cash flow at 20%. The answer is as follows:

	£			£
Investment	(10,000)	×	1.0000	(10,000)
1	5,000	×	0.8333	4,167
2	4,000	×	0.6944	2,778
3	2,000	×	0.5787	1,157
4	2,000	×	0.4823	965
5	1,000	×	0.4019	402
NPV				(531)

Thus we have two calculations, one which shows a positive NPV at 10% cost of capital and the other which shows a negative NPV at 20% cost of capital. Between these two points there must be a rate – between 10% and 20% – that brings the NPV down to zero. This rate is the IRR.

How is this rate calculated?

These days it comes automatically out of a computer spreadsheet or programmable calculator. Before these were available it had to be done by iteration and this method is shown here to demonstrate the principles involved.

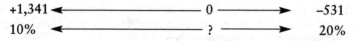

It can be seen visually that the point where zero is crossed on the way from £1,341 to (£531) is in the late teens, somewhere around 16% or 17%. This can be confirmed by an interpolation calculation; the total range from £1,341 to (£531) is £1,872 so the calculation will be:

$$\frac{£}{1,341} \times 10\% = 7.16\%$$
$$\frac{1,341}{1,872} \times 10\% = 7.16\%$$

Thus zero is crossed 7.16% of the way along the line between 10% and 20%, so the apparent break-even rate is 17.16%.

Is it accurate to interpolate in this way?

No, it can be inaccurate to quite a large extent so this method is only to be used as a way of getting closer to the actual percentage. Now that we have established that the IRR is around 17%, we should try to prove it by discounting at 17% and seeing what the NPV will be at that level.

	£			£
Investment	(10,000)	×	1.0000	(10,000)
1	5,000	×	0.8547	4,274
2	4,000	×	0.7305	2,922
3	2,000	×	0.6244	1,249
4	2,000	×	0.5337	1,067
5	1,000	×	0.4561	456
NPV				(32)

This calculation shows that, though the initial interpolation indicated an IRR of just over 17%, the actual IRR must be just below. There is a negative NPV of £32 at 17% so the IRR which achieves break-even must be slightly lower than this.

What will the NPV be at 16% discount rate?

This is a necessary calculation to arrive at the final IRR and it looks like this:

	£			£
Investment	(10,000)	×	1.0000	(10,000)
1	5,000	×	0.8627	4,310
2	4,000	×	0.7432	2,973
3	2,000	×	0.6407	1,281
4	2,000	×	0.5523	1,105
5	1,000	×	0.4761	476
NPV				145

This shows that the IRR is closer to 17% than 16% and you could do an exact calculation (which a spreadsheet will do and which we could now do mathematically) but a number to the nearest 1% is all that is required. Anything more precise would be misleading in view of all the assumptions that have to be made in building up the cash flows of project evaluations.

OK, so now we know that the IRR is around 17%, what does that mean to a manager looking at a project?

The IRR is saying that, even if the cost of capital/discount rate were to be as high as 17%, we would still break-even on this project. Another way of expressing this is to say that, if the cost of capital is (say) 10%, there is an excess or safety margin over the cost of capital of 7% (17 − 10).

We know that the word INTERNAL is meaningless, but what of the word RETURN? In what sense is this percentage a return on investment?

Effectively the IRR is the average cash return over the life of the project. The reason for this is easier to see if you think about the further meaning of the initial explanation of IRR above. *If you are saying that you can break-even while the cost of capital is 17%, you must also be saying that the project is making 17% before financing costs.*

taking it further

This section gives details of relevant and useful resources and contacts.

Books and other reading

MTP novels

The Bottom Line, Alan Warner (Aldershot, Gower)
Beyond the Bottom Line, Alan Warner (Aldershot, Gower)
Before the Bottom Line, Alan Warner and Simon Woolley (Aylesbury, MTP)
Improving the Bottom Line, Alan Warner and Simon Woolley (Aylesbury, MTP)

MTP Management Briefing Series

Financial Reporting, Alan Warner (Aylesbury, MTP)
Investment Appraisal, Alan Warner (Aylesbury, MTP)

Teach Yourself Series

Teach Yourself Finance for Non-Financial Managers, Philip Ramsden (London, Hodder Education, 2008)
Teach Yourself Setting up a Small Business, Vera Hughes and David Weller (London, Hodder Education, 2006)
Teach Yourself Small Business Accounting, David Lloyd (London, Hodder Education, 2006)
Teach Yourself Understanding Tax for Small Businesses, Sarah Deeks (London, Hodder Education, 2006)

Other reading

Financial Management for the Small Business (London, Kogan Page)

Websites

Business Link: **www.businesslink.gov.uk**

Chambers of Commerce: **www.britishchambers.org.uk**

The Chartered Institute of Management Accountants: **www.cimaglobal.com**

Federation of Small Businesses (FSB): **www.fsb.org.uk**

HM Revenue & Customs: **www.hmrc.gov.uk**

The Institute of Chartered Accountants in England and Wales: **www.icaew.co.uk**

The authors may be contacted via their website (**www.mtpplc.com**) or by email on **learn@mtpplc.com**.

acid test   The ratio of liquid assets – cash and debtors – to current liabilities; used to assess the credit worthiness of a business. Also called 'Quick Ratio'.

acquired goodwill   The amount paid for the intangible assets of a business as a result of an acquisition, calculated as the excess of price paid over the value of Balance Sheet assets.

assets   The value of items owned by a business as shown in its Balance Sheet.

Balance Sheet   A financial statement that records assets, liabilities and shareholder investment in a business at the end of an accounting period.

bank draft   A method of organizing invoice payment whereby the paperwork is made available through the banking system, once the customer has confirmed instructions.

Base Rate Loan   A loan arrangement whereby the interest rate varies with the base rate set by the Bank of England (or equivalent in other countries).

below the line   P&L items that are not connected with operations and are shown below the Operating Profit line, for example, Interest, Taxation and Dividend.

book value   The value at which assets are stated in the Balance Sheet.

business model   The ways in which a business carries out its operations, which have an impact on its financial structure.

business plan   A statement of what the management of a business intends to do over a future period, and the expected outcomes.

capital Amounts of money raised to fund a business over the long term (also used as an alternative term to describe Capital Expenditure – see below)

capital budget An estimate of the amount to be spent on capital expenditure in a future accounting period.

capital expenditure Amounts spent on assets that have a benefit beyond the current year, and are not therefore treated as immediate costs in the P & L.

capital intensity The extent to which a business requires a high proportion of capital expenditure to carry out its operations.

capital repayment holiday An agreement between borrower and lender for repayments on a loan to be temporarily suspended.

cash account The position of the bank account as shown in the accounting records of a business.

cash balance The amount of cash held by a business at the end of an accounting period

cash flow The change in the cash position of a business during an accounting period.

cash flow forecast A forward projection of the likely cash flow position in the future, based on best estimates of cash in and out.

cash flow from financing activities Cash flow arising from changes to financial structure and payments of dividend to shareholders

cash flow from investing activities Cash flow arising from the investment in, and disposal of, Fixed Assets

cash flow from operating activities Cash flow generated by the normal operations of a business, after changes in Working Capital but before investment and disposal of Fixed Assets

cash flow statement A document which sets out the cash flow of an accounting period and shows the changes that have taken place in the cash position.

competitive advantage The ways in which a business can deliver products or services that are superior to others in the market.

Corporation (Corporate) Tax Taxation levied on businesses, based on the profit made in a particular accounting period.

cost of capital The average cost of raising capital for a business, taking into account the existing cost of debt and equity finance, and the proportions of each.

Costs Amounts of expenditure of a short-term nature which are charged to the P&L Account, because they refer to the operations of the current accounting period.

creditor ratio The level of creditors at the end of an accounting period, expressed as a ratio to the sales or cost of sales of the same period.

creditors Amounts owing to suppliers for invoices unpaid at the end of a financial period.

current assets Those short-term assets that will be converted into cash during the next 12 months, i.e. stocks, debtors and cash.

current liabilities Amounts owing at the period end that will need to be paid within the next 12 months, i.e. creditors, tax owing and bank overdraft.

debt The amount of a company's funding that consists of borrowed money.

debtors Amounts owing by customers at the end of an accounting period.

depreciation A book entry that spreads capital expenditure over its estimated life, thus creating a cost which reduces profits in the P&L Account.

Discounted Cash Flow (DCF) An approach to evaluating projects that involves discounting projected future cash flows back to today's values.

discount factor The factor used to convert future cash flows into present values, based on the assumed cost of capital.

Discounted Payback A variation on the Payback method of investment evaluation, which involves the calculation of the time required to recover the initial outlay, using present value figures.

discount rate The rate at which the cash flows of a project are discounted, to arrive at present values.

dividend Amounts of cash paid to shareholders as a distribution of profits.

earnings Profit available to shareholders after all charges except dividend. In more general language, Earnings can also be used as an alternative term for profit at all levels.

equity The amount of a company's funding that consists of investment by shareholders.

expenses Another term for costs, normally applied to those that are not part of the direct costs of the product.

factoring An arrangement whereby the debtors of a business are sold to a specialist organization in return for an agreed fee.

financial accounting The processes that result in the production of the three financial statements – Balance Sheet, Cash Flow statement and P&L.

financial lease A lease that involves the provision of finance to obtain a Fixed Asset and does not provide any other benefits to the lessee.

financial plan A forward projection of all three financial statements – Balance Sheet, Cash Flow statement and P&L – providing the financial outcome of the business plan.

fixed assets Those assets that have been purchased and are retained for long-term use in the business.

fixed costs Costs where the total amount spent will be the same, whatever the level of sales volume.

Fixed Rate Loan A loan arrangement whereby the interest rate is set at a fixed level, irrespective of the base rate set by the Bank of England or equivalent.

free cash flow The amount of cash left for shareholders after deduction of all cash flows except their own dividend distribution and share buybacks.

funds flow A method of arriving at cash flow by starting with profit and then adjusting for all the differences between cash and profit.

GAAP Generally Accepted Accounting Principles as laid down by statutory and accounting bodies in a particular country.

gross profit The level of profitability after product costs have been deducted from sales.

incremental cash flow The impact of a decision on the cash flow position of a business, as used to evaluate investment projects.

intangible assets Fixed Assets that cannot be physically touched or recognized, such as trademarks, brands and acquired goodwill.

Internal Rate of Return A method of evaluating investments, requiring the calculation of the 'break-even' discount rate that will bring the Net Present Value back to zero.

Letter of Credit A form of guaranteed payment that allows invoices to be settled earlier, in return for a discount taken by the bank.

liquid assets Assets that can be converted into cash relatively easily, i.e. debtors, cash and cash equivalents.

liquidity ratio The ratio of Current Assets to Current Liabilities; used to assess the credit worthiness of a business.

liabilities Amounts owed by a business to third parties at the end of an accounting period.

loan capital Long-term capital invested in a business by lenders rather than shareholders.

management accounting   Financial information produced for the purpose of management decision making and control.

marginal cost   The extra cost incurred as a result of a decision, ignoring the allocation of existing fixed costs.

matching principle   An accounting principle that requires costs to be matched with sales in each accounting period, to arrive at the best possible definition of profit.

MBA   Master of Business Administration

Net Present Value (NPV)   A method of evaluating investments, requiring the calculation of the net value of the project cash flow, after discounting at the agreed cost of capital.

net stock ratio   The excess of stock over creditors at the end of an accounting period, expressed as a ratio to the sales or cost of sales of the same period.

non-notified factoring   A type of factoring whereby the customers of the business are not told about the existence of the arrangement.

non-recourse factoring   A type of factoring whereby the risk of non-payment is transferred to the factoring organisation.

notified factoring   A type of factoring whereby the customers of the business are told about the existence of the arrangement.

off Balance Sheet   A term applied to arrangements which are designed specifically to keep the financial realities off the published Balance Sheet.

Operating Cash Flow   The cash flow generated by a business after Capital Expenditure and changes in Working Capital have been deducted. (Can also be defined as after working capital but before capital expenditure.)

operating expenses   Costs incurred that can be attributed directly to business operations.

operating lease   A lease that provides finance to obtain a Fixed Asset, along with other operational benefits to the lessee, for example maintenance services.

operating profit   The amount of profit made on business operations, before deduction of 'Below the Line' items like Interest, Tax and Dividends.

overdraft   A facility for short-term borrowing available from banks to cover cash flow requirements during peak periods.

payback   A method of evaluating investments, requiring the calculation of the time it takes for the initial outlay to be recovered.

present value The value of a future cash flow, discounted back to its equivalent value today.

private equity Shareholder finance obtained from private investors rather than from a public share issue.

profit The excess of sales over costs of a business during an accounting period.

Profit and Loss Account (P&L) A financial statement that measures the performance of a business by recording the sales, costs and profit for an accounting period.

provision An estimate made to include costs in the P&L Account, on occasions when the amount to be incurred is not yet clearly established.

quick ratio The ratio of liquid assets – cash and debtors – to current liabilities; used to assess the credit worthiness of a business. Also called 'Acid Test'.

recourse factoring A type of factoring whereby the risk of non-payment stays with the company selling its debtors.

revenue expenditure Another term for costs in the P&L Account, distinguishing these from longer-term Capital Expenditure.

sale and leaseback An arrangement whereby the Fixed Assets of a business are sold to a property company and then leased back for an agreed charge and period.

sales The amounts charged for goods or services delivered to customers in an accounting period.

shareholders Those who invest money in a business and become part owners, entitled to receive a share of dividends.

stock The amount of cash spent on products or services that have not yet been sold; consisting of raw materials, Work-in-Progress and finished goods.

stock ratio The stock at the end of an accounting period, expressed as a ratio to the sales or cost of sales of the same period.

tangible assets Fixed Assets that can be physically touched and recognized, such as land, buildings, machinery and equipment.

Treasury Loan A loan arrangement with the bank for amounts over £100,000, whereby repayments are tailored to the cash flow of the business.

Triple A rating A classification provided by credit rating agencies, saying that the business concerned has the best possible ability to repay a loan with minimal risk.

Value Added Tax (VAT) A tax system which is related to sales and costs, where the net amount of cash owing has to be paid to the tax authorities each quarter.

working capital The amount of cash tied up in stocks and debtors, less the amount that is financed by suppliers via non-payment of creditors.

index

teach yourself

small business accounting
mike truman and david lloyd

- Are you new to small business accounting?
- Do you want to run your business more effectively?
- Do you want a reliable way of controlling your finances?

Small Business Accounting provides practical guidance on how to keep the books and prepare the accounts for your small business. Forget about debits and credits, journal entries, ledgers and day books – if you can read a bank statement this book will teach you how to prepare accounts, make forecasts of your cash flow and prepare a budget.

David Lloyd is an award-winning Chartered Accountant who advises hundreds of business clients. He has been delivering real-world business finance training for many years.

setting up a small business
vera hughes and david weller

- Are you setting up a small business?
- Do you need help to define what you have to offer?
- Are you looking for guidance in marketing and finance?

The best-selling **Setting up a Small Business**, now in its fourth edition, gives you clear, concise information and guidance in all aspects of setting up a small business, including legal requirements, IT, finance and staffing issues.

Vera Huges and **David Weller** started their own business in 1980 and have wide experience of many areas of commerce. In addition to the phenomenally successful **Setting up a Small Business** they have written a number of books on retailing.